THE TRUTH BEHIND
BEHIND
the Secret

JAMES K. WALKER
BOB WALDREP

HARVEST HOUSE PUBLISHERS

EUGENE, OREGON

Cover by Dugan Design Group, Bloomington, Minnesota

THE TRUTH BEHIND THE SECRET
Copyright © 2007 by James K. Walker and Bob Waldrep
Published by Harvest House Publishers
Eugene, Oregon 97402
www.harvesthousepublishers.com

Library of Congress Cataloging-in-Publication Data
Walker, James K.
The truth behind the secret / James Walker and Bob Waldrep.
    p. cm.
ISBN-13: 978-0-7369-2298-2 (pbk.)
ISBN-10: 0-7369-2298-9 (pbk.)
    1. Byrne, Rhonda. Secret. 2. Success. 3. Spiritual life—Miscellanea. 4. Apologetics. I. Waldrep, Bob. II. Title.
    BF1999.W22743 2007
    131—dc22

                                                                    2007015502

Printed in the United States of America

07 08 09 10 11 12 13 14 15 / VP-SK / 12 11 10 9 8 7 6 5 4 3 2 1

Acknowledgments

We would like to take this opportunity to thank some of those who helped to make this book possible. We greatly appreciate our wives, Debra Waldrep and Jimmie Walker, who endured our late nights at the office and patiently postponed family time while we were researching and writing. We are also very thankful for the wonderful staff at Watchman Fellowship for their help. Some put in countless extra hours of hard work to free us up to be able to complete the book. Others, such as Phillip Arnn, senior researcher, and Preston Condra, associate director, helped with the research, fact checking, and interviews.

A special word of thanks needs to be expressed to the scientists, researchers, authors, and experts who agreed to be interviewed for this book, including:

Dr. Erica Carlson (Ph.D., UCLA) assistant professor of physics, Purdue University.

Marj Hartman (M.A. in apologetics, Simon Greenleaf University) research assistant, Reasons to Believe, Pasadena, Calfornia.

Dr. Jon Klimo (Ph.D., Rosebridge Graduate School) faculty, PsyD Clinical Psychology Program, Argosy University (San Francisco bay area campus). Author of *Channeling: Investigations on Receiving Information from Paranormal Sources.*

Bryan Lankford, a leading Wiccan high priest in the north Texas Pagan community, cofounder of the OIC coven, and author of *Wicca Demystified.*

Dr. Robert L. Park (Ph.D. in physics, Brown University) professor of physics, University of Maryland.

Dr. Hugh Ross (Ph.D. in astronomy, University of Toronto) president and director of research, Reasons to Believe, Pasadena, Calfornia.

Dr. Richard Sloan (Ph.D., New School for Social Research) professor of behavioral medicine (in psychiatry) at the Columbia University Medical Center.

Finally, we would like to express our deep appreciation for the hard work, patience, and encouragement of Steve Miller, senior editor at Harvest House Publishers.

CONTENTS

FOREWORD

The Secret by Rhonda Byrne is not just another positive thinking, you-can-have-it-all, self-help, New Age, or metaphysical book. While similar books have become increasingly prominent since the 1980s, this book is different. Unlike its predecessors, *The Secret* has had an unparalleled impact in the general market, having become a runaway bestseller in both print and video formats. In fact, within just a few months of publication, the book alone had sold well over a million copies. Why?

The Secret makes very beautiful and powerful promises. They are promises that are just too important to ignore. If true, *The Secret* could be the missing key that solves the world's most perplexing problems, the answer to life's most burning questions, and the ultimate fulfillment of every human yearning.

The Secret claims to be both ancient and new. Although her book was published just last year, Rhonda acknowledges that *The Secret* is not new information. It is actually thousands of years old. For centuries, Byrne says, her secret has been silently practiced by the world's most wealthy, famous, and successful people. She maintains that this same secret has also been hidden in the ancient scriptures and teachings of the world's great religions. It's also new. Byrne teaches that her secret is a relatively new finding for modern science. Byrne claims that recent scientific discoveries—particularly related to quantum physics—have now proven her secret. *The Secret* is both an ancient, universal law and a modern scientific discovery.

Others agree. Byrne acknowledges that she found over 50 modern-day authors, experts, and teachers who are writing about or teaching this very same "secret." Even Oprah Winfrey has admitted to using its principles (though not calling it the secret) for over 20 years. No doubt, the promises it offers and Oprah's affirmation and devoting two editions of *The Oprah Winfrey Show* to *The Secret* have greatly contributed to the book's unrivaled success and the intense fascination with its teachings.

But there is much more to *The Secret* than most readers are aware. In fact, there are some very significant secrets behind *The Secret*. With millions now reading, watching, and spreading *The Secret*, we need to know:

- *What is this "secret," and why is it so appealing?*

- *What is the real source of this secret and how does this affect the scientific and spiritual claims of* The Secret*?*

- *What is the truth behind* The Secret*?*

This book will help you answer these and other crucial questions. It investigates and explores the remarkable claims and principles of *The Secret* and its teachers. Finally, this book gives you uncensored access to the truth behind *The Secret*—particularly its source, its science, and its appeal to sacred traditions.

WHAT IS *THE SECRET*?

Unhappy with your love, your job, your life, not enough money? Use your head. You can think yourself into a lot better you. Positive thoughts can transform, can attract the good things you know you want. Sound far-fetched? Think again. It's supported by science.[1]

LARRY KING, TALK SHOW HOST OF
CNN's *LARRY KING LIVE*

In February of 2007, publishing giant Simon & Schuster announced the largest reprinting in their history for the runaway bestseller *The Secret* by Rhonda Byrne.[1] Earlier that month both the book and the DVD it was based upon shot to the top of the best-seller lists, supplanting *Harry Potter and the Deathly Hallows*. Even though the book was out of stock, both versions of *The Secret* still climbed to first place at Amazon.com.

Interest in *The Secret* has truly exploded. Byrne reports that within a few months of the release of the DVD, enthusiastic followers began to hold Secret parties in homes around the world. Universities and schools began sharing the secret with their students, and churches of all denominations began sharing it with their members.[2]

Even Oprah Winfrey has helped to spread the secret. Oprah's first program on *The Secret* received such a huge response that eight days later she aired an unprecedented follow-up show called "One Week Later: The Huge Reaction to *The Secret*." The book and DVD have also been featured on a variety of network talk shows, including CNN's *Larry King Live* and *The Ellen DeGeneres Show*.

Amazingly, Simon & Schuster's record two-million-copy reprint order came just three months after the book was released. It brought the total number of copies in print to a staggering 3.75 million.[3] This does not include the 1.5 million copies sold of the DVD version. This is truly remarkable for a first book written by an obscure Australian television producer.

How could an unknown author generate this kind of excitement and attention? What is attracting millions of loyal readers and viewers? What is the secret behind *The Secret*?

The Secret promises to be the source of everything your heart desires— and more. Do you yearn for tranquility, financial security, strengthened relationships, or perfect health? Would you like to lose weight? Do you need a convenient parking spot at a busy mall, or would you like world peace? The keys to everything you have ever wanted—personal well-being, prosperity, and harmony—are all promised in *The Secret*. It is your Aladdin's Lamp, whose genie does not limit you to just three wishes because *"there's absolutely no limit whatsoever to the wishes."*[4]

Blog sites have sprung up on the Internet filled with testimonials about the positive power of *The Secret* to change lives. Amanda's story, featured on *The Oprah Winfrey Show,* is typical of this kind of anecdotal evidence that *The Secret* really does work. After 16 years of marriage, Amanda and Mark say they were at a breaking point in their relationship. "I was exploding with anger and had just had enough," Amanda says. Within 24 hours of watching the episode on *The Secret,* Amanda says her entire outlook on life changed. "I think that we have a miraculous chance of moving forward and having a great life together."[5]

Some of the testimonials are so enthusiastic they seem to rival ecstatic religious experiences. One satisfied customer on Barnes & Nobles' Web site claimed the book provided "a glimpse into the higher planes of our celestial realm."

> *This book has literally changed my universal perception!! The Secret is the most joyous and rapturous journey that any mere mortal can possibly experience in our spiritual sphere of existence. The metaphysical ramifications of the book's mind-blowing philosophies transcend the limits of consciousness and allow the reader a glimpse into the higher planes of our celestial realm.... I now have a vacation home in the Bahamas, a jet ski.... Next week I plan to learn to fly!*[6]
>
> A BARNES & NOBLE CUSTOMER REVIEW

Indeed, *The Secret* promises not only physical riches and happiness, but it is a spiritual message as well. According to the book, this secret has a positive religious message taught by Jesus Christ and the Bible. Furthermore, the message of *The Secret* was purportedly known and taught by the world's great religious teachers, including Moses, Buddha, Mohammed, Gandhi, and in the scriptures of Hinduism. Byrne claims that her research discovered "religions, such as Hinduism, Hermetic traditions, Buddhism, Judaism, Christianity, and Islam and civilizations, such as the ancient Babylonians and Egyptians, delivered [*The Secret*] through their writings and stories."[7]

This, then, is the secret. It is the elusive answer to the eternal yearning of all humankind. Buried here is the key to the spiritual goals of peace, harmony, and awareness coupled with the very practical desires of financial riches and physical health.

- *Is this too good to be true, or is it something real?*
- *Could Rhonda Byrne's discovery really change the world?*
- *Can an ancient secret contain this much power?*

Before you can begin to answer these questions, someone will have to share with you "the secret."

THE SECRET SHARED

We all work with one infinite power. We all guide ourselves by exactly the same laws…. we're all working with one power. One Law. It's attraction!

The Secret is the law of attraction!

Everything that's coming into your life you are attracting into your life. And it's attracted to you by virtue of the images you're holding in your mind.[1]

BOB PROCTOR, PHILOSOPHER, AUTHOR, AND PERSONAL COACH, WHAT IS "THE SECRET" AND HOW DOES IT WORK?

Rhonda Byrne was given her first glimpse of the secret in the spring of 2004 when she was at one of the lowest points in her life. A divorced mother in her 50s, Byrne remembers, "I'd worked myself into exhaustion, my father died suddenly, and my relationships with my work colleagues and loved ones were in turmoil."[2]

With her life out of control and on the verge of desperation, Byrne had no warning that everything was about to change. It was at that critical time that she first heard the secret. It came into her life in the form of an obscure, 100-year-old book[3] she received from her daughter Hayley. Life would never be the same.

> *Something inside of me had me turn the pages one by one, and I can still remember my tears hitting the pages as I was reading it.... It gave me a glimpse of The Secret. It was like a flame inside of my heart. And with every day since, it's just become a raging fire of wanting to share all of this with the world.*[4]
>
> RHONDA BYRNE

Rhonda's mind raced. Why had it taken over 50 years for her to learn of this? Why didn't the whole world know these marvelous principles?

She discovered that some of the world's most important historical figures had been guardians of the secret, including Plato, William Shakespeare, Sir Isaac Newton, Hugo, Ludwig van Beethoven, Abraham Lincoln, Ralph Waldo Emerson, Thomas Edison, and Albert Einstein.

Although it had existed throughout history, Byrne became convinced that the secret had been suppressed. Ruthless institutions and greedy tycoons, for their own corrupt reasons, had conspired to keep the secret to themselves. The common folks were suppressed and subjugated. Wars and poverty resulted all because the secret had been lost...or had it?

Byrne dropped everything and began a search. Were there living oracles of the secret? If so, who were these living masters and how could she find them? She was confident that she would be guided to them by the principles of the secret that she had already learned. The search would very quickly take her from her home in Australia to the United States.

As a professional television producer, Byrne had a dream to use her media talents to bring the secret to the masses. She had financed and pulled together a capable video team to document her discoveries. Byrne's entire crew, Prime Time Productions, left for the States with no real clue of where they would find these masters.

> The day that the Prime Time Productions team arrived in the United States to film the living masters of The Secret, they only had one interview lined up. But they brought with them an entire crew and the firm intention that they would film every person they needed for the movie. And in a matter of a few weeks, the team filmed a total of fifty-two "teachers" of The Secret. Wherever the team went, more and more amazing teachers would emerge— great writers, leaders, philosophers, doctors, and scientists. These teachers created the foundation for The Secret.[5]
>
> RHONDA BYRNE

Within a few months, the team crafted the raw footage into a 91-minute documentary. When early plans for a television broadcast were thwarted, however, Byrne turned to Internet distribution and a highly successful marketing campaign. The results were staggering. According to ABC News, one of the masters featured in The Secret called the launch of the DVD the greatest moment in history. "This is the most historic moment in history because this powerful information is being broadcast to the masses, to the people on the street in a way they can understand and relate to," Joe Vitale told ABC News. "They sit. They watch it. They absorb it."[6]

Both the DVD and downloadable versions of the video are still selling through Byrne's Web site, but the real explosion took place when Byrne was approached by Simon & Schuster with a book deal followed by appearances on *Larry King Live* and *The Oprah Winfrey Show.*

Millions now know the secret, and thousands more are learning the secret every day. But exactly what is Rhonda Byrne's secret?

LET ME TELL YOU A SECRET

The secret can be summarized in this simple phrase: "Thoughts become things."[7] Whether positive or negative, good or bad, whatever a person thinks about, concentrates on, or visualizes will eventually become reality.

Do you find yourself always worried about bills? Your mind in harmony with that ancient unchangeable secret law begins to attract more debt. Intentionally focus on positive thoughts of prosperity, and the universe will begin to align itself in such a way as to channel income your way.

Byrne insists this is not just wishful thinking. In fact, *The Secret* argues that through quantum physics, science has already proven the principle on a subatomic level. Its power comes from an eternal, inexorable law—a secret principle—called the Law of Attraction.

Through teaching, drama, and testimony, Byrne and her roster of experts set forth the principles of the Law of Attraction. Thoughts, we learn, function like powerful magnets. Positive thoughts attract positive results and negative thoughts draw negative results.

At its heart, the Law of Attraction is a very simple yet bold and provocative claim. The human mind has an intrinsic, virtually unlimited ability to literally change the physical world.

Thoughts become things.

Your thoughts are the secret source of an unimaginable, infinite power when properly fueled by positive emotion and released in three simple steps: ask, believe, and receive.[8]

According to the secret, thoughts work like a powerful television transmission tower. Thoughts actually vibrate at predetermined frequencies broadcasting from your mind. That mental signal reaches out into your immediate surroundings, around the world, and even into the farthest reaches of the universe.[9] That transmission does not produce a mere television picture or sound—it produces every element of that tangible, physical environment that we call reality.

You don't believe it? Well, that's why it will not work. That is the Law of Attraction. You are broadcasting your doubts and lack of faith right back to yourself, and those thoughts are being manifested right now before your eyes. Properly change your thinking, and you have forever mastered the secret key to everything you ever dreamed or desired.

LET ME GET IN YOUR FACE

The bad news is that everything going wrong in your life today is actually your fault. The source of your problems is you—or at least your own wrong thinking.

> *Everything that surrounds you right now in your life, including the things you're complaining about, you've attracted. Now I know at first blush that's going to be something that you hate to hear. You're going to immediately say, "I didn't attract the car accident. I didn't attract this particular client who gives me a hard time. I didn't particularly attract the debt." And I'm here to be a little bit in your face and to say, yes you did attract it. This is one of the hardest concepts to get, but once you've accepted it, it's life transforming.[10]*
>
> JOE VITALE, SECRET TEACHER

According to the Law of Attraction, there are no truly innocent victims. Every apparent victim, from starving children in Haiti to Holocaust casualties in Germany, was personally responsible for attracting their negative experiences. They did it to themselves because of their own wrong thinking. Apparently Joe Vitale would be in the face of 9/11 survivors saying, "Yes you did attract this." The bad news is that you only have yourself to blame.

But the *Secret* teachers would not want you to be discouraged, so think of it this way: The bad news is also the good news.

Armed with the secret, you have the principles and the power to turn it all around and change everything for the better. It is the secret to that new sports car, the perfect mate, a better job, and that dream vacation.

You need not stop there. Once you fully understand and correctly master the secret, you have also discovered the panacea for every incurable disease, including cancer,[11] and you have discovered the elusive key to world peace. All is made possible through the secret Law of Attraction.

Once you learn the secret, you are responsible. And quite naturally, you probably have some important questions:

- *Isn't this just wishful thinking, or is there more to it?*
- *Does* The Secret *raise some ethical or spiritual questions?*
- *What harm could there be in trying it?*

Let's find out by meeting some of *The Secret*'s cynics.

3

THE SECRET CYNICS

But here's the thing. It doesn't matter what kind of press the Secret and the Law of Attraction receive. Remember, the Law of Attraction says that what you focus on expands.

When the NY Times runs a negative article about the Secret what are they focusing on? When CBS sets up a debate...what are they focusing on? When CNN runs a snarky story on the Secret what are they focusing on?

Every time the Secret and/or the Law of Attraction appear in the mainstream press, regardless of how positive or negative the coverage is, it is truly a blessing because it brings this information into the awareness of more people.[1]

EDWARD MILLS, LAW OF ATTRACTION COACH,
TEACHER, SPEAKER, AND WRITER

What's not to like? The secret Law of Attraction could be the key to human happiness. Who has not desired personal prosperity, physical well-being, or world peace? It is also a spiritual message that has supposedly been hidden in the sacred writings of Christians, Jews, Muslims, and Hindus. Thus, the message of *The Secret* should bring personal happiness and enhance rather than conflict with everyone's existing spiritual beliefs regardless of his or her religion.

Yet in the midst of its wild popularity, booming sales, and breathless testimonials, *The Secret* has drawn a surprising backlash of criticism. Ironically, the Law of Attraction is manifesting significant detraction. Some in the media are urging caution, while others say it is not true and its claims are fraudulent. Even some religious leaders are going public with warnings about its message.

Jerry Adler, writing for *Newsweek* magazine, says, "On an ethical level, 'The Secret' appears deplorable."[2] *USA TODAY* quotes Syracuse University professor Robert Thompson, a professor of media and popular culture, who calls *The Secret* " 'at best, silliness.' It's 'good old American snake-oil salesmanship.' "[3]

In a scathing review in *Salon* entitled, "Oprah's Ugly Secret," Peter Birkenhead writes, "By continuing to hawk 'The Secret,' a mishmash of offensive self-help clichés, Oprah Winfrey is squandering her goodwill and influence, and preaching to the world that mammon is queen."[4]

> *It would be stupidly dangerous to dismiss Oprah and "The Secret" as silly, or ultimately meaningless. They're reaching more people than Harry Potter, for God-force's sake. That's why what Oprah does matters, and stinks. If you reach more people than Bill O'Reilly, if you have better name recognition than Nelson Mandela, if the books you endorse sell more than Stephen King's, you should take some responsibility for your effect on the culture. The most powerful woman in the world is taking advantage of people who are desperate for meaning, by passionately*

> *championing a product that mocks the very idea of a meaningful life.*[5]
>
> • PETER BIRKENHEAD, "OPRAH'S UGLY SECRET," *SALON*

In some cases, supporters of *The Secret* are also raising red flags. Dr. Joe Siegler, M.D., shared some of his concerns with the *Chicago Sun-Times*:

> The book and DVD give examples of cancer patients who laughed and positive-thought their way back to good health—and that troubles Siegler, who also is a medical doctor. "They're starting to sell snake oil at that point," says Siegler, who otherwise is a "Secret" fan. "The medical piece is almost like a sick person would be blamed if they don't get over [his disease]…."[6]

The story in question is the testimony of Cathy Goodman, a cancer survivor who shunned chemotherapy and radiation treatments and allegedly used the Law of Attraction to heal herself. Part of her self-treatment included reducing stress by watching funny movies to "just laugh, laugh, and laugh." She shares her unshakable faith in the secret:

> I was diagnosed with breast cancer. I truly believed in my heart, with my strong faith, that I was already healed. Each day I would say, "Thank you for my healing." On and on and on I went, "Thank you for my healing." I believed in my heart I was healed. I saw myself as if cancer was never in my body.[7]

Bob Proctor, one of the teachers heavily featured in *The Secret,* is also somewhat uncomfortable with the inclusion of Goodman's story in *The Secret.* When interviewed on ABC's *Nightline,* he said that he personally was not recommending that cancer patients replace doctor-prescribed treatment with *The Secret.* He explained, "If I was diagnosed with cancer I'd be the first to go and take whatever treatment they gave me."[8] He did acknowledge, however, that *The Secret* might imply otherwise. He admitted that if he had written *The Secret* he "probably would not" have included Goodman's story.[9]

DON'T SHOW ME THE MONEY

Cynics are also critical of Byrne's focus on money. Richard Hooper complained of the DVD's obsession with wealth and personal happiness, saying, "I watched all of five minutes of the 'movie' before becoming totally bored." He called it "Positive Thinking for Dummies."[10] Hooper is no stranger to the principles touted in the DVD. He was the principal sound recordist for the late Earl Nightingale,[11] who was the personal mentor of *The Secret* star Bob Proctor.

Joe Vitale, another key teacher featured in *The Secret*, expressed some uneasiness with its unrelenting materialism, saying,

> "I love 'The Secret' but I also think it's missing a couple things," says "metaphysician" Joe Vitale. "If I were producing it, I would have added something more about serving others." Vitale defends the dream homes and sports cars as baubles to draw people in, in hopes they will employ the law of attraction for higher purposes.[12]

Critics claim that the focus of *The Secret* is not on the "higher purposes." It's about expensive necklaces, sports cars, and attracting checks to your mailbox. It's mostly about "stuff." And if the focus is on material wealth, does that not create some logical and ethical contradictions? Ingrid Hansen Smythe, writing for the Skeptics Society, makes this same observation when she asks, "…if everybody knows *The Secret*, won't there be a mad dash for all the good stuff and no one will get anything?"

Smythe then sarcastically adds,

> Not to worry. Not everyone wants the same things, we are told—and here there is a visual of an Indian snake charmer, followed by a little Chinese woman in a boat with a bunch

of domestic fowl. Apparently, the Indian man and the Chinese woman don't *want* a car....

Add to the above the following quote: "Wise people have always known this.... Why do you think that 1% of the population earns around 96% of all the money that's being earned?... It's no accident. It's designed that way.... They understand *The Secret.*" Ah, there it is then. It is the *wise* people who have the money and the BMWs. Are we to conclude that the Indian man and the Chinese woman are fools? The deeply offensive racial overtones are hard to ignore, as are the sexist slurs.... Evidently social inequality and injustice, a lack of resources, several thousand years of patriarchy, oppression and inequality between the sexes—all the usual explanations as to why people don't have money are incorrect. Social factors are irrelevant in a world where "*You* are the *only* one who creates your reality. It is only you; every bit of it you."[13]

Incompatible with Major Faiths

Perhaps Rhonda Byrne could expect a fair amount of criticism from the secular media and professional skeptics. A chorus of criticism, however, is also coming from religious leaders—people of faith. A wide variety of them contend that the message of *The Secret* is not found within their sacred writings, as Byrne claims.[14] Not only is the secret not in their scriptures, they believe it is incompatible with their faith.

An editorial published by Catholic Online warns that *The Secret* offers only "false happiness" and denies the book's implicit claim that the "Catholic Church worked assiduously through the centuries to keep 'The Secret' a secret."[15] Mitch Pacwa, a Jesuit priest who hosts the popular Catholic TV program *EWTN Live,* called *The Secret* "an old scam" and "New Age nonsense dressed up for TV."[16]

A number of evangelical Christians have also been critical of *The Secret*. Donald S. Whitney, Ph.D., an associate professor of biblical spirituality at the Southern Baptist Theological Seminary, states, "It is no exaggeration to say that this book implicitly (and sometimes explicitly) denies virtually every major doctrine in the Bible."[17]

Citing several passages from the Qur'an, Sunni Muslim teacher Imam Hassan Kahlil finds no common ground between Islam and the message of *The Secret*. He explains that "the whole Qur'an from A-Z is loaded with completely the opposite, and to be honest with you I find [*The Secret*] very ludicrous."[18]

When asked about *The Secret*, Bryan Lankford, a leading Wiccan practitioner in the North Texas Pagan community, was careful not to criticize Rhonda Byrne. He did point out, however, that from his perspective, there was nothing new in *The Secret*. His own 2005 book *Wicca Demystified* teaches the Law of Attraction using very similar terminology: "thoughts are things."[19]

> *Wicca teaches that thoughts are things; this is one of the basic principles of magick. We view that our thoughts have energy which travel from us into the world causing changes in our environment. Everything we think about sends energy out into the world which changes the world in some way. Most thoughts don't have enough energy behind them to actually do much, but some will set a chain of events into motion which will lead to something magickal happening in one's life.* [20]
>
> BRYAN LANKFORD, AUTHOR, *WICCA DEMYSTIFIED*

Some Jewish leaders have been very critical of *The Secret*. Writing for Aish HaTorah,[21] Rabbi Benjamin Blech complains, "*The Secret* simply doesn't work—and for very good reason. God wasn't foolish enough to create a world blindly responsive to human cravings." Blech explains that the Law of Attraction is not compatible with Judaism. "It suggests that

God is a cosmic bellhop just waiting to grant every one of our wishes if we only believe strongly enough that He'll do it...."[22]

The news media, literary critics, cultural commentators, and religious leaders from a wide variety of faiths are raising objections to *The Secret.*

The temptation here is to simply dismiss them all as just so much irrelevant negativity. These criticisms, however, do raise some important questions that warrant our attention:

- *With* The Secret *helping so many people, how can anyone respond negatively?*

- *Do these criticisms work to offset the very principles of* The Secret?

- *Could there really be some "dark side" to* The Secret?

We cannot know the answers to these questions until we uncover the mysteries surrounding a woman named Esther Hicks, a being (or group of beings) called "Abraham," and the secret source behind *The Secret.*

THE SECRET SOURCE

If you have the ability to imagine it, or even to think about it, this Universe has the ability and the resources to deliver it fully unto you.... And within every particle of this Universe is that which is wanted and the lack of it. This perspective of abundance, and the lack of it, is the environment in which focus is possible—and focus activates the Law of Attraction.[1]

ABRAHAM, A GROUP CONSCIOUSNESS
FROM THE NONPHYSICAL DIMENSION[2]

Most fans of *The Secret* DVD will be surprised to learn that they have not actually seen *The Secret*—at least, not the original one. Rare copies of the first edition of the DVD are not available at Barnes & Noble or at Rhonda Byrne's Web site. These hard-to-find first editions of *The Secret* have been selling on eBay and Amazon.com for over $100.

Some of the early fans of the original video are less than thrilled with the current, edited version, which has now sold over 1.5 million copies. This popular version is called the extended edition. It's not the extended portions that are causing controversy, however, but what was edited out.

The original video is known as the Abraham-Hicks edition. Hicks is a reference to Esther Hicks, a 58-year-old woman who may be considered the leading teacher of the original DVD. Abraham is somewhat more difficult to explain.

According to Hicks, Abraham is an entity, or more accurately, a collection of several nonphysical entities who have been in personal contact with her for over two decades.

> *Abraham is not a singular consciousness as you feel that you are in your singular bodies. Abraham is collective consciousness. There is a stream or river of consciousness. As one of you asks a question, there are many, many points of consciousness that are funneling through what feels to be one perspective (because there is, in this case, one human, Esther [Hicks], who is interpreting or articulating it), so it appears singular to you. We are multidimensional and multi-faceted, and certainly multi-consciousness.*[3]
>
> ABRAHAM

Whereas Rhonda Byrne discovered the secret in 2004, Esther and her husband Jerry have been teaching the Law of Attraction for over 20 years. They currently travel the country in a $1.4 million luxury tour bus conducting Law of Attraction workshops in hotel ballrooms and charge $195 for each ticket.[4] They also host Caribbean, Hawaiian, and Alaskan "Well Being" cruises featuring the wisdom of Abraham.[5] They have authored more than 600 products, including publications, audio teachings, and videos.

One of their current bestsellers is the book *The Law of Attraction: The Basics of the Teachings of Abraham.*

Esther Hicks is called the "star" of *The Secret* by early fans of the original edition.[6] When comparing the original version with the extended edition, it becomes apparent that Hicks did play a fundamental role in the initial project. Almost everything shared by Hicks in the original edition is also found in the Hickses' earlier book *Ask and It Is Given,* published in 2004 by Hay House.

This book, like their others, is primarily channeled information from Abraham. The Library of Congress Cataloging-in-Publication Data for the book states "Abraham (Spirit), Ask and it is given: learning to manifest your desires / [channeled by] Esther and Jerry Hicks."[7]

Hay House distributed *Ask and It Is Given* in Australia through Hay House Australia, and it is possible that Byrne had been exposed to the book before coming to the United States to film *The Secret.* In the official press release, Byrne states that she had only one interview scheduled in advance before the whole production team came to the United States.[8] Byrne never names that person, but Hicks's role in the original edition, coupled with the parallels between *The Secret* and *Ask and It Is Given,* leads one to wonder if Abraham's teachings in the Hickses' book was the catalyst that brought Byrne and the production team to America.

The royalties offered to the Hickses were also substantial. Initially Rhonda Byrne must have felt Abraham's role was critical to the video, because she offered Esther Hicks 10 percent of the profits for her participation.

That contract and its lucrative royalties were jeopardized, however, when strong disagreements developed over the video's style and content.[9]

BAD VIBRATIONS: SECRET PROMISES BROKEN

According to a report published in *The New York Times*,[10] initially Jerry and Esther Hicks were given a good deal of control over *The Secret*. But when the couple screened a preproduction copy of the video, they were "livid" over the fact that Esther was missing. Although Esther's voice could be heard narrating *The Secret*, her face was never shown.

A full-blown conflict was avoided and a compromise reached when the video was edited to include footage of Mrs. Hicks's face before the video was released. The Hickses received half a million dollars in royalties from that first edition, even though it received relatively little distribution. Then more trouble developed.

Although the Hickses have disputed portions of the story,[11] *The New York Times*[12] reported that further conflict ensued concerning video distribution and royalties. The Hickses were displeased when the initial agreement to premiere *The Secret* on Australian television failed to materialize and Byrne started selling Internet downloads instead. Eventually lawyers got involved and the Hickses received a "loving" letter that, according to the couple, notified them that "the contract that we had all agreed upon and signed was no longer sufficient for their further distribution of the project." The Hickses were informed "that it would be necessary for us (Jerry and Esther) to relinquish our intellectual property rights in these areas forever" or they would be edited out of future videos.[13]

Esther Hicks said she had never seen anyone leverage the Law of Attraction like Rhonda Byrne. "I've never seen anybody do that like she's doing it…. And never mind honesty, and never mind doing what you said you were going to do, and never mind anything. Just stay in alignment."[14]

The best-known teacher featured in *The Secret*, Jack Canfield, was brought in to try to mend the rift. Canfield, best-selling author of the Chicken Soup for the Soul book series, was unable to mediate a compromise between Byrne and the Hickses. Byrne followed through on her promise and produced the new extended edition of the video, editing out both the face and voice of Esther Hicks/Abraham.

For the most part, the teachings of Hicks (or rather Abraham) are retained (in some cases almost verbatim) in the new version, with the narration of other *Secret* teachers (mostly Lisa Nichols and, in some cases, Marci Shimoff) replacing the voice of Hicks. Mr. Hicks, a former Amway distributor, said that despite their attorney's advice, they decided not to sue Byrne because that would not be in harmony with their own focus on the Law of Attraction.

Many bloggers who are longtime fans of Abraham-Hicks are discouraged by these developments while trying to stay positive. For example, Helga Finken, who has gone on two cruises with Abraham, says, "I was sort of sorry to hear about Jerry and Esther's 'problems' with the people who produced 'The Secret.'.... The movie wouldn't be the same without Abraham." [15] Others have also lamented the decision to remove Hicks, expressing bitter disappointment. Still others have vowed not to purchase the new Hicksless edition.

> *I have to say...that's a huge bummer. [Esther Hicks] glows in that movie and everyone I have showed it to was so wonderfully taken by her. It was nice to show it to people who may have otherwise been very closed to abe [Abraham] material. They saw her and listened, and melted.* [16]
>
> DANA UNDERWOOD, *SECRET* BLOGGER

> *[Esther Hicks] is being edited out of* The Secret.... *I e-mailed the support staff of* The Secret *website specifically to make sure she'd be in the DVDs I purchased. No way was I going to pay for it without her. She made the film for me, really. Not to downplay the contributions of the others, but her parts are what stuck out most to me and the film would not have the same impact without her.* [17]
>
> PEACEFUL BLADE, *SECRET* BLOGGER

Millions of readers have now purchased the book, watched the current edition of the video, and seen Rhonda Byrne on *Oprah*. The vast majority are unaware of the important role played by Abraham-Hicks and know nothing of the subsequent controversy. The only allusion to the Hickses' original role is a brief reference to "Jerry and Esther Hicks and the teachings of Abraham" found in the acknowledgments section of the book near the end of a long list of over 80 people who inspired or assisted Byrne.[18]

BUT WHO OR WHAT IS ABRAHAM?

Perhaps a positive consequence of Hicks (Abraham) being edited out of the current edition of *The Secret* is it virtually eliminates that thorny "Abraham question." Had Esther Hicks remained in the current, wildly popular edition of *The Secret,* millions would have naturally wondered, "Just what or who is Abraham?" or more accurately, "What or who *are* they?"

The Hickses describe Abraham not as a single being, but a collection of nonphysical entities, "a group of obviously evolved teachers, [who] speak their broader Non-physical perspective through the physical body of Esther."[19]

> *Physical human has found many labels that they use, depending on how they feel in the moment, to try to describe their interaction with Nonphysical. We are Source Energy. We are Collective Consciousness...meaning a stream. We are a consensus of many (what you might call) Nonphysical voices. We are that which some have called angel. We are that which some have called God. We are that which some have called Inner Being. But most importantly (and we'll use some of our favorite words again) we are focalized Consciousness, specifically responding to the vibration that you manage in your asking.[20]*
>
> ABRAHAM

Abraham, according to the Hickses, is a composite entity made up of a number of individuals or personalities existing in some kind of nonphysical or spiritual dimension. These teachers or avatars have chosen to use the physical body and voice of Esther to share their messages with the world. For over two decades, Esther Hicks has functioned as a medium or channel for these spirit beings.

So now we know another secret. Hicks (or if you prefer, Abraham) was the "secret source" of the original edition of *The Secret*. In that edition, it was Abraham speaking through the voice of Esther Hicks who shared the mysteries of the Law of Attraction. That law is the focus of the Hickses' book *The Law of Attraction: The Basic Teachings of Abraham,* which was featured on the *New York Times* best-seller list for over six weeks in 2006.[21] This, however, does not answer the bigger question: Who or what is Abraham?

OUR NAME IS ABRAHAM

In their earlier book *Ask and It Is Given,* the Hickses describe how they first met Abraham. Esther shared that in the early years of their marriage, she was disturbed by the stories her husband told about his experiences with the Ouija board in the 1960s. She felt so uncomfortable with his graphic descriptions she would often excuse herself from the conversation due to a strong fear of anything that might be evil or connected with the devil.[22]

She was eventually able to overcome those fears.

In 1984, at her husband's request, the couple visited a woman named Sheila who "speaks with spirits." They met Sheila in a beautiful home in Phoenix, Arizona. A tape-recorded session was conducted in which Sheila relaxed, released her consciousness, and began breathing very deeply.

Suddenly a strange-sounding voice began speaking through the mouth of Sheila, saying, "It is the beginning, is it not? You have questions?"[23]

The voice coming from Sheila was identified as Theo, a "Non-Physical entity." Esther shared that she was "*not* ready to talk with whoever was now speaking" to them. Jerry, however, was more than ready. For the next half hour, Jerry plied Theo with questions he had pondered since childhood.

By the end of the session, Esther's fears had vanished. During a second visit with Sheila, Esther began to ask some of the questions. It was during that second session that Esther began to be taught the value of meditation and affirmation. She was advised to begin using meditation techniques coupled with an affirmation, which included summoning "Beings" to give her enlightenment. Hicks still remembers that specific affirmation.

> *I [Esther Hicks] see and draw to me, through divine love, those Beings who seek enlightenment through my process. The sharing will elevate us both now.*[24]
>
> ESTHER HICKS, CHANNELER OF ABRAHAM

Esther says that upon hearing that affirmation, she experienced a feeling of love that flowed to the core of her being. It was in that same session that she learned some astonishing news. Speaking through Sheila, Theo informed Jerry and Esther that they too were channels and that they would soon learn the name of their "spiritual guide" through a clairaudient experience.[25]

Returning home that evening, Esther and Jerry began to experiment with meditation. Esther focused on trying to find out the name of her spiritual guide. She describes what came next:

> ...I closed my eyes and began to breathe consciously....then I counted my breath, in and out, in and out. Right away, my entire body felt numb. I couldn't distinguish my nose from my toes. It was a strange but comforting sensation and I enjoyed it. It felt as if my body was slowly spinning even though I knew that I was sitting in a chair....
>
> [Later,] I felt numbness overtake my entire body. But this time, something, or someone, began to "breathe my body." From my vantage point, it felt like rapturous love, moving

from deep inside my body outward. What a glorious sensation! Jerry heard my soft sounds of pleasure and later said that, to him, I appeared to be writhing in ecstasy.[26]

After the session, Esther's teeth were chattering so rapidly she described them as "buzzing." While she didn't learn their name at the time, she now knows this was her first contact with Abraham.

The Hickses continued similar meditation practices on a daily basis for the next nine months when suddenly a new phenomenon developed. Esther began to feel her head begin to move very gently from side to side during meditation sessions. After three days of this, it suddenly dawned on Esther that her head movements were definitely not random. Her nose was actually spelling out alphabet letters. Instantly, Jerry grabbed a notebook and began to write what Esther was spelling: "I AM ABRAHAM. I AM YOUR SPIRITUAL GUIDE." [27]

Over the next few weeks, messages from Abraham began to flow through Esther. Writing with her nose, however, was somewhat slow and awkward. One night, under Abraham's influence, Esther felt a strong impulse to place her hands on her typewriter. Seemingly, of their own accord, her hands began to move across the keyboard without her conscious effort. To her surprise, the typewriter clacked out the following message:

> I am Abraham. I am your spiritual guide. I am here to work with you. I love you. We will write a book together.[28]

They did more than write a book together. Automatic writing through the typewriter eventually gave way to direct, verbal channeling. Abraham was able to use Esther's voice to communicate messages that they preserved in hundreds of hours of audio recording and countless pages of transcripts.

It was that voice, the voice of Abraham speaking through Esther Hicks, that Rhonda Byrne captured in her original video.

The basic teaching of Abraham was and is the secret—the Law of Attraction.

It was that secret, Abraham's secret, that Rhonda Byrne made public in her *New York Times* number one best-seller.

ADDITIONAL SECRETS

The basic teaching of Abraham is the Law of Attraction, but he has (or they have) shared many additional messages on countless subjects. Readers of *The Secret* would certainly want to know what other teachings are coming from Abraham through Hicks.

For years the Hickses have provided weekly recordings from the voice of Abraham to subscribers who pay $12 per month. The Hickses also publish these teachings in books, audio recordings, and a journal. Excerpts are also available online.[29]

Most of the Abraham-Hicks teachings relate directly or indirectly to the Law of Attraction. Much advice is given on trusting one's emotions and feelings as a barometer to measure alignment with that law through what is called the Emotional Guidance System.

These teachings also place an importance on the understanding and use of vibrations and nonphysical energy. The reality of physical matter seems to be of secondary importance, if not illusionary, in comparison. Ultimately, humans are nothing but pure, positive energy.

According to Abraham, emotions help one to link with that energy or connect with one's God force.

> *Every time you turn around there's somebody else saying, "Come this way." "No. Come this way." Or, "Whatever you do, don't go that way." And it is so wonderful when you finally connect, when you finally get the correlation that elation means you're connected to your God Force and anger means you're not.*[30]
>
> ABRAHAM

It is beyond the scope of this book to provide a comprehensive summary of all of Abraham's teachings. It may be surprising, however, to learn that not all of Abraham's secrets are positive and uplifting.

Many humans who may be described as "less highly evolved" may find some of his secrets to be quite frightening. Those who are less spiritually evolved should be aware of an approaching spiritual Darwinism.

THE JURASSIC SECRET

Abraham's message to humans is that in their current, unenlightened state, they are facing imminent extinction as a species. Humankind must learn the message of the dinosaurs—the Jurassic Secret.

According to Abraham, prehistoric dinosaurs learned to modify their surroundings using their power of imagination. When interviewed by a conference guest, Abraham confirmed his earlier teachings. It was actually dinosaur visualization that allowed for the evolution of human life. In a section entitled "Dinosaurs R us, as us R?" Abraham explains:

> **Guest**: Abraham, you've said that dinosaurs, which preceded us, imagined and altered their environments, which then allowed the rise of the human being. Is it the case that humans are now imagining and preparing earth's environment for the next iteration of the leading edge life form?
>
> **Abraham**: Yes. And it will be an expanded, evolved, more eager, more exhilarated, more stable, more healthy, more focused, more satisfied, more creative human.
>
> **Guest**: If that's the case, then is the destination of that human the result of some kind of plan? Is there something that's guiding us in a certain direction?
>
> **Abraham**: No, it's not a master plan in the sense that something has already been decided. It's the natural by-product of an environment, which continues to evoke, on

many levels of every human being, new preferences. So the fantastic, positive, forward moving evolution must take place. It is the inevitability of the Well-being. Future generations will look back on that which you now are, as a species, and call you Neanderthal by comparison. They will talk of times when humans did not understand emotions. And they will talk of times when people boldly blundered forward doing things just for the sake of pleasing others, rather than satisfying self and ultimately connecting with Source Energy.

They will talk of those who saw with only their five senses. "They could see and hear and taste and smell, and touch, but they had not begun to consciously develop that broader sense of reading vibration and therefore understanding the true nature of every moment in their life experience."

Oh, there is so much delicious stuff before you! And much of it you will experience as soon as tomorrow, if you like.[31]

RESISTANCE IS FUTILE?

Abraham also provides a "birth and death" warning to those who reject this vision of a new and better world. For the doubters who are not "allowing" this new world order, "resistance is futile."[32]

> There are those who believe that the world is getting more and more desperate. We are here to tell you that the world is getting better and better, and better, and that every experience you have causes you to launch rockets of desires, and Source comes in response to those. And the best thing about your birth and death is that the resistant ones die and the allowing ones are born.[33]
>
> ABRAHAM

Undoubtedly, once readers of *The Secret* learn of the Esther Hicks connection, many will be drawn to seek out all the additional teachings of Abraham. For other fans however, questions about Abraham's other teachings will probably be eclipsed by a more fundamental curiosity.

- *Are the entities called Abraham real, living beings?*

- *Is Hicks's contact with nonhuman immaterial entities or communication with the spirits of dead people a product of her subconscious mind?*

- *How can we explain or understand this phenomenon called channeling?*

Our curiosity will start being satisfied as we begin to deconstruct the secret séance.

THE SECRET SÉANCE

For at least 2500 years, and across virtually all countries, cultures, and peoples, one can find many thousands of examples of individuals who claim, or who have claims made of them, that they are receiving information and messages from beings or spirits who exist on some other level of reality than our own here on Earth.

Some of these communicating sources are said to be human beings not currently possessing human bodies (discarnate), including those who have gone through the process of physical death and survive in some trans-physical realm. Some of these non-physically based beings are said to be non-human, ranging from angels and various other spiritual beings to nature spirits, from extraterrestrials to other-dimensionals, from gods to demons.[1]

DR. JON KLIMO, LEADING EXPERT ON THE PHENOMENON
OF CHANNELING, AUTHOR OF *CHANNELING*

As we have seen, the secret source of the concepts found in the original edition of *The Secret* is Abraham, who speaks through a woman named Esther Hicks. Abraham is declared to be a composite of a group of disembodied beings, or "a consensus of many (what you might call) Nonphysical voices."[2]

Most people's exposure to channeling today is limited to caricatures portrayed by Hollywood and television. Many may think of the character Oda Mae Brown, a channeler played by Whoopi Goldberg in her Academy Award-winning performance for the 1990 movie *Ghost.*

To get a more accurate perspective on this source of *The Secret,* we need to get a better frame of reference.

WHAT IS CHANNELING?

There are at least five basic possibilities or explanations for the phenomenon of channeling:

1. Some believe channeling is simply a dramatic variation of a séance, in which the medium not only contacts the dead but also allows the deceased spirit to enter into and use the channeler's body.

2. Others believe that real, nonphysical entities are entering the channel but they are not and have never been human. They are believed to be avatars, spirit guides, or aliens operating on some higher, nonphysical, immaterial plane.

3. A number of psychologists and psychiatrists have suggested a wide variety of possible psychological explanations (both normal and abnormal). Some channeling could be symptomatic of a variety of mental illnesses or perhaps a tapping into some Jungian archetype or collective unconsciousness.

4. Bible scholars have suggested that some channeling may involve evil, fallen angels (known as demons) who can

impersonate dead people or spirit guides in what amounts to a form of demon possession.[3]

5. Skeptics have charged that channeling is nothing more than fakery, with the medium simply pretending to channel some being, sometimes with the help of various forms of stage magic, cold reading, or other forms of deception.[4]

To discuss these possibilities, we interviewed Dr. Jon Klimo, considered by many to be the world's foremost authority on channeling. His 1988 book *Channeling: Investigations on Receiving Information from Paranormal Sources* (revised and updated in 1998) is widely considered to be *the* definitive work in that field.

Personally, Klimo is a firm believer in channeling and regularly practices a form of that communication that he calls "open channeling."[5] He expressed regret that the Abraham-Hicks material was edited out of *The Secret* but agreed to discuss current theories pertaining to channeling and the controversial nature of the subject.

Klimo has done extensive historical research on channelers and mediums and investigated hundreds of examples of contemporary channeling. He defines the phenomenon as follows:

> Channeling is the communication of information to or through a physically embodied human being from a source that is said to exist on some other level or dimension of reality than the physical as we know it, and that is not from the normal mind (or self) of the channel.[6]

THE TECHNIQUES USED BY CHANNELERS

Klimo identifies nine basic techniques employed by channelers: They include full trance, sleep channeling, dream channeling, light trance, clairaudient channeling (supernaturally hearing the spirits), clairvoyant channeling (supernaturally seeing the spirits), automatisms (automatic writing, typing, or Ouija board), open channeling (no specific entity identified), and physical channeling (moving or materializing physical objects).

Klimo personally believes many channeled communications are real and helpful messages coming from actual spirit beings. He does not, however, rule out purely psychological explanations for some channeling and devotes a whole chapter to various psychological theories.[7]

He also readily acknowledges that he believes some channeling is fraudulent.

> *[Some channeling] is only nonsense, an entirely self-generated phenomenon, which very often involves conscious or unconscious fakery. It is true that the claims of some channels have been found to be without merit. We must keep in mind, therefore, that this subject is fraught with possibilities of deception and misunderstanding.*[8]
>
> JON KLIMO, AUTHOR OF *CHANNELING*

THE DANGERS OF CHANNELING

Most interesting is Klimo's warning about evil spirits in connection with channeling. As a proponent and practitioner of channeling, Klimo is familiar with the traditional Christian perspective that fallen angels (demons) may be involved. Although Klimo does not completely agree with this perspective, he readily acknowledges that some channeling does involve evil beings bent on deception.

In his interview, he explained, "not every ancient spirit is wise or benevolent"—some belong to "the dark brotherhood." Klimo repeatedly referred to these dark beings as spirits who are involved in some kind of invisible warfare against all that is good. While he believes these evil spirits are in the minority, he recognizes a significant potential danger when it comes to channeling, noting, "[There are] even more dangerous sources...

nonhuman demons, evil spirits, forces of Satan or Lucifer and the 'Dark Brotherhood.' These entities await every opportunity to tempt and control human spirits. Historically, the negative presence of lower astral human spirits has been attributed to these demonic entities."[9]

If we accept Klimo's explanations of channeling, then we have to acknowledge that deception is possible. There is the possibility of fraud and fakery, self-deception on the part of the channeler, a mental illness or psychological phenomenon, or even an evil, demonic spirit pretending to be a wise helper.

Ultimately, Klimo's insights raise more questions. So what do we do with Abraham, channeling, and the secret source of the Law of Attraction? How do we put all this in context? How do we evaluate *The Secret*?

Those who are confused by or are uncomfortable with the idea of spirit communication from nonphysical entities could choose to simply ignore the source of the secret and look to the science. After all, regardless of what one thinks about channeling or the enigma of Abraham, the scientific claims made in *The Secret* are impressive.

- *What does it matter where it came from as long as it really works?*

- *Does it really work, and if so, how?*

- *Do scientists, doctors, and quantum physicists support the scientific claims made in* The Secret?

The answers to these questions will be revealed as we begin decoding the science behind the Law of Attraction and uncover the secret "bleep."

THE SECRET "BLEEP"

I'm not talking to you from the point of view of wishful thinking or imaginary craziness. I'm talking to you from a deeper, basic understanding.

Quantum physics really begins to point to this discovery. It says that you can't have a Universe without mind entering into it, and that the mind is actually shaping the very thing that is being perceived.[1]

DR. FRED ALAN WOLF, QUANTUM PHYSICIST, LECTURER, AND AWARD-WINNING AUTHOR FEATURED IN *THE SECRET* AND *WHAT THE BLEEP DO WE KNOW!?*

One of the most impressive claims made by *The Secret* is that it is not some unproven theory based on "imaginary craziness." The Law of Attraction is presented as a universal, unchanging principle that is backed up by science. Not just any science, but what Rhonda Byrne calls "new science."

That new science is quantum physics, and these scientific principles are said to transcend the older Newtonian laws of a cause-and-effect universe. When properly understood and applied according to the principles of *The Secret,* this science challenges traditional thinking and revolutionizes everything from medicine and disease to weight loss and diet. Quantum physics proves the secret. On a subatomic level, "thoughts become things."

Thus, the laws of the universe that comprise *The Secret* are not founded merely on spiritual claims. Rhonda Byrne can prove *The Secret* from science. What are the new discoveries in quantum physics, and how do they support the medical and scientific principles of the Law of Attraction?

WHAT THE BLEEP DO WE KNOW!?

To discover the science behind the secret, we need to go back a few years. The year is 2004, the same year that Rhonda Byrne first discovered the secret. It was then that an unusual documentary was released, *What the Bleep Do We Know!?*[2]

The Secret seemed to rely very heavily on this earlier documentary. Both films make virtually identical claims concerning quantum physics. They both make the same claim that there is scientific evidence that human thought can attract, change, or create matter.

In fact, the two physicists Byrne chose for *The Secret,* Dr. John Hagelin and Dr. Fred Alan Wolf, had already appeared in *What the Bleep!?* making similar scientific claims.

While many of the same scientific declarations are made in both films, the earlier documentary is more detailed. Rather than just making the claims, *What the Bleep!?* actually tries to explain and illustrate the underlying scientific principles.

The stated goal of *What the Bleep!?* is to reunite science and religion—the secular and the sacred. Like *The Secret*, the core of the earlier film is a series of interviews with experts. A key component of their teaching is that science has now proven that consciousness or thought affects, changes, or even creates the material universe.

The film includes a fictional drama about a troubled photographer named Amanda, who is played by actress Marlee Matlin. Amanda struggles with everything from negative memories of failed relationships to emotional concerns about her weight and the size of her thighs. By the end of the documentary, Amanda has learned about subatomic anomalies, parallel universes, and the illusionary nature of distance and time. She learns the secret behind the amazing power of the mind to create out of nothing using only thought. She also discovers the practical benefits that can be derived from this knowledge, including good health, perfect weight, and healed relationships.

THE SECRET CONNECTION

There is another—and quite surprising—connection between the two films. Before evaluating the science behind *The Secret* and *What the Bleep!?* we have to acknowledge and deal with this other very remarkable coincidence.

It is channeling.

Like *The Secret* (original edition), *What the Bleep!?* relies heavily on channeled communication. In this case, it is not Esther Hicks but JZ Knight, founder of JZK, Inc. and Ramtha School of Enlightenment in Yelm, Washington.

Knight, born Judith Darlene Hampton, channels a 35,000-year-old warrior named Ramtha, who is from the lost land of Lemuria.[3] Two

decades ago, *Time* magazine identified Knight as the most famous channeler of the day.

> Probably the most celebrated of all current channelers is
> J.Z. Knight, a handsome ex-housewife in Yelm, Wash., who
> has performed for thousands at a price of $150 each per
> session. She speaks for Ramtha, a 35,000-year-old warrior
> who reports that he once lived on Atlantis. He has even dic-
> tated a book, I Am Ramtha, published in Portland, Ore., by
> Beyond Words Publishing and illustrated with photographs
> of Knight going into a trance on The Merv Griffin Show.[4]
>
> OTTO FRIEDRICH

I AM RAMTHA THE ENLIGHTENED ONE, INDEED

Ramtha first appeared to Knight and her husband in their mobile home
in 1977. Over the next three decades, Knight's companies generated millions of dollars in revenue marketing the wisdom of Ramtha. Through
out-of-body experiences, Knight says she can temporarily make room in
her body for Ramtha, who then lectures and teaches using Knight's body
and vocal cords.[5] Ramtha marks his arrival with the announcement, "I
am Ramtha the Enlightened One, indeed."[6]

JZ Knight appears throughout *What the Bleep!?* as Ramtha, speaking
with an unusual accent while sharing philosophical wisdom, discussing
the science of quantum physics, and teaching principles that parallel
Byrne's Law of Attraction.

> But we always wonder then, don't we? When we wish for
> all of us to be able to heal with a touch and to raise the
> dead and to manifest a loaf of bread in our hand. We
> always wonder why we can't do that but we can never
> ask a question that we don't already know the answer to.

> *And the answer is, it is because we don't believe we can do it....*[7]
>
> RAMTHA

Knight, who is not initially identified, seems to function throughout the film in the role of a scientist or some kind of spiritual philosopher. In the credits, she/he is identified as "Ramtha, master teacher, founder of the Ramtha School of Enlightenment, channeled by JZ Knight." Interestingly, the three principal filmmakers of *What the Bleep Do We Know!?* were students at the Ramtha School of Elightenment.

THE DALAI LAMA

Another spiritual documentary released in the summer of 2007 features a reunion of some of the teachers from *The Secret* and *What the Bleep!?* Shot in the Himalaya mountains of northern India, *Dalai Lama Renaissance* documents a meeting of 40 "innovative thinkers" summoned by the spiritual leader of Tibetan Buddhism to help solve the world's problems.[8]

Invited by the Dalai Lama for the meeting and film were Fred Alan Wolf (featured in both *The Secret* and *What the Bleep!?*), Amit Goswami from *What the Bleep!?* and Agape Church founder Michael Bernard Beckwith, one of the main teachers in *The Secret*.[9]

Did *What the Bleep!?* help inspire *The Secret*? *What the Bleep!?* appears to set forth virtually all the scientific theories later used in *The Secret*, and two of the same scientists appear in Byrne's 2006 video.

Whatever influence *What the Bleep!?* might have had on Rhonda Byrne in 2004 may never be known. The parallels—including content and participants—seem too significant to be mere coincidence.

The most remarkable coincidence, the one that is the most difficult to ignore, is that both videos heavily featured the channeled teachings of nonphysical entities—Ramtha and Abraham.

How does this affect the credibility of the scientific claims in both films? Channeling does not sound very scientific; it sounds very religious.

For many, communicating with ancient spirits who take over human bodies may sound like science fiction or something from the movie *Ghostbusters*. Others may conclude that channeling has more in common with the occult than science. Some may also see all this talk of metaphysical consciousness and spirit channeling as a challenge to their existing religious beliefs. What happened to the science?

JZ Knight/Ramtha seems to anticipate the uneasiness of many who are attempting to understand the message scientifically but are put off by the channeling. The spirit communication is a real hot potato that injects religious, spiritual, and "cultish" overtones into the teachings.

> *Do you think science will understand that better than having to handle a hot potato called consciousness that has so much cultish, religion, backwater Voodoo attached to it?*[10]
>
> RAMTHA

It is a hot potato, indeed—one that raises all kinds of questions about the underlying nature of the secret Law of Attraction.

- *Is the Law of Attraction a scientific discovery proven by quantum physics or a religious belief taught by spirit beings?*
- *Could it be both?*
- *Can we set aside the religious issues and just focus on the science?*

To find these answers, we must first learn the science of the secret.

THE SECRET SCIENCE

The law of attraction is the law of creation. Quantum physicists tell us that the entire Universe emerged from thought! You create your life through your thoughts and the law of attraction, and every single person does the same. It doesn't just work if you know about it. It has always been working in your life and every other person's life throughout history. When you become aware of this great law, then you become aware of how incredibly powerful you are, to be able to THINK your life into existence.[1]

RHONDA BYRNE, AUTHOR OF *THE SECRET*

Some might say we should not necessarily reject the message of *The Secret* merely because we cannot understand or accept the idea of the spirit beings or the practice of channeling. If the message of *The Secret* is true, it should be embraced regardless of its source. Indeed, the Law of Attraction tantalizes us with the possibility of solving virtually every human need—from poverty and disease to world peace. If there is even a remote possibility that it is scientifically true, we cannot afford to ignore it.

It does not matter if this message comes from Abraham, Ramtha, or some other disembodied spirit or even from a Chinese fortune cookie—as long as it works. That is the power of *The Secret*. You don't have to believe in spirits, because modern science has now proven the Law of Attraction.

> *When I discovered The Secret, I wanted to know what science and physics understood in terms of this knowledge. What I found was absolutely amazing. One of the most exciting things about living in this time is that the discoveries of quantum physics and new science are in total harmony with the teachings of The Secret, and with what all the great teachers have known throughout history.*[2]
>
> RHONDA BYRNE

Discovering the science behind *The Secret* is no easy task. In fact, separating the spiritual and religious aspects of *The Secret* from the science is more difficult than might first be imagined.

Many of the experts who make scientific claims throughout *The Secret*, such as Bob Proctor and Rhonda Byrne, are not scientists. Most of the leaders quoted in the book have no graduate degrees or formal training of any kind in quantum physics.

The teachers of *The Secret* include Reverend Michael Beckwith, a New Thought pastor who was ordained as a minister in Religious Science,[3] and Marie Diamond, a feng shui[4] consultant. *Secret* teacher Neale Donald Walsch is a "spiritual messenger,"[5] whose best-selling book *Conversations with God* was whispered into his right ear in a channeling-like process that he likens to "dictation."[6]

Many of the teachers in *The Secret* are motivational speakers, "visionaries," ministers, or spiritual leaders, not scientists. (These will be discussed in more detail in later chapters.) This "spirit/science entanglement" makes it difficult to separate hard scientific statements made by real experts from the unsubstantiated opinions of untrained amateurs.

Two of the experts featured in *The Secret*, however, are scientists who are familiar with subatomic properties and have formal training in the field of quantum physics. They are Fred Alan Wolf, who holds a Ph.D. in theoretical physics (author of *The Yoga of Time Travel: How the Mind Can Defeat Time*) and Dr. John Hagelin, who has a Ph.D. in physics from Harvard and worked at CERN (the European Center for Particle Physics) in Switzerland.

Even when limiting the discussion to the physicists in *The Secret*, it is hard to avoid additional religious baggage.

THE "SCIENCE" OF YOGIC FLYING

Dr. Hagelin is perhaps the best-credentialed scientist in *The Secret*. He has a number of political as well as scientific achievements. In 1996 he received 110,000 votes as a United States presidential candidate representing the Natural Law Party,[7] which he cofounded.

Dr. Hagelin's early scientific achievements and political ambitions have not created much of a stir. What has been the topic of much controversy is his religious conversion. He became a follower of the Maharishi Mahesh Yogi and left his position at the Stanford Linear Accelerator Center in 1984 to join the faculty of Maharishi University in Fairfield, Iowa.

The Maharishi is the founder of Transcendental Meditation (TM), who gained world recognition when he became the personal guru to the

Beatles in the mid-1960s. Despite claims to the contrary, TM has been ruled to be a religious practice by the U.S. courts and has been barred from public schools.[8]

The Maharishi and Dr. Hagelin both believe in something called yogic flying.

TM meditators believe that through proper training, they can defy the law of gravity and actually fly using only the powers of their minds. In public demonstrations, they have only been able to produce "stage one" flying, which is called hopping. It is said that eventually, followers will be able to demonstrate the other two stages—hovering and flying around in a room.

Dr. Hagelin believes that TM-trained yogic flyers have the mental powers to reduce or prevent terrorism, crime, war, poverty, and positively affect the stock market.[9]

Steve Twomey of the *Washington Post* described a demonstration of stage-one yogic flying as "bouncing like dropped marbles."

> *No tricks: no wires, no ropes, no drugs, no propellers or jetpacks, merely the power of the human mind breaking the bounds of gravity. Or so it would seem....Wait. He's up again. Now down. And up. All the others are doing it too, bouncing like dropped marbles. To the uninitiated, it looked less like flying and more like 13 men in the lotus position painfully hopping across 67 foam pads.*[10]
>
> STEVE TWOMEY

As in *The Secret*, most of the experts featured in *What the Bleep!?* who make scientific statements lack serious academic credentials in the corresponding field of study. Masaru Emoto, for example, is a doctor of alternative medicine and Joseph Dispenza is a chiropractor. Michael Ledwith, Ph.D., now a teacher at Ramtha's School of Enlightenment, is a former professor of systematic theology at Maynooth College in Ireland.[11]

What the Bleep!? does, however, feature real scientists with degrees in physics, in addition to John Hagelin and Fred Wolf from *The Secret.*

GETTING BLEEPED OUT

At least one of those scientists, however, has come forward accusing the makers of *What the Bleep!?* of deceptive editing and misrepresentation. David Albert, professor and director of Philosophical Foundations of Physics at Columbia University, "is outraged at the final product,"[12] claiming the filmmakers twisted his interview to fit their agenda. In fact, he patiently and clearly explained why consciousness could not be linked with quantum physics, but that portion of his interview was edited out.

> *"I don't think it's quite right to say I was 'tricked' into appearing,"* he said in a statement reposted by a critic on What the Bleep's *Internet forum, "but it is certainly the case that I was edited in such a way as to completely suppress my actual views about the matters the movie discusses. I am, indeed, profoundly unsympathetic to attempts at linking quantum mechanics with consciousness. Moreover, I explained all that, at great length, on camera, to the producers of the film.... Had I known that I would have been so radically misrepresented in the movie, I would certainly not have agreed to be filmed."*[13]
>
> DAVID ALBERT

While Dr. Albert does not believe there is a link, some scientists apparently do believe that quantum mechanical theories support the Law of Attraction. Dr. Fred Alan Wolf and Dr. John Hagelin, who are featured in both films, seem to really believe that science has proven *The Secret.*

WHAT ARE SCIENTISTS REALLY SAYING?

When examining the scientific claims of Wolf and Hagelin (as well as the nonscientists in *The Secret*), it is important to understand that the theories and views in no way represent the scientific community as a whole. These individuals are expressing views considered to be on the outer limits of the fringe by mainstream academia.

We felt it would be extremely helpful to have scientists, professors, researchers, and physicists independently evaluate the scientific statements of fact found in *The Secret*. When we scheduled interviews for this book we discovered many of the individuals who were recognized as experts in these fields of study did not want their names associated with Rhonda Byrne or *The Secret*. Off the record, however, every one of them who were contacted expressed either dismay or incredulity when hearing quotes from *What the Bleep!?* and *The Secret*.

Fortunately, several scientists and researchers were willing to be interviewed on the record for this book. They are...

- *Erica Carlson* (Ph.D., UCLA with postdoctoral research at Boston University)—Assistant professor of physics, Purdue University, specializing in condensed matter theory of strongly correlated electronic systems.

- *Marj Hartman* (M.S., University of Arizona, and M.A. in apologetics, Simon Greenleaf University—master's thesis "Does Quantum Physics Prove that Observer Determines Reality?")—Research assistant, Reasons to Believe, Pasadena, California.

- *Robert L. Park* (Ph.D. in physics, Brown University)— Professor of physics (former chairman) at the University of Maryland, and Director of Public Information, Washington office of the American Physical Society.

- *Hugh Ross* (Ph.D. in astronomy, University of Toronto with postdoctoral studies at Caltech, researching quasi-stellar objects)—President and Director of Research, Reasons to Believe, Pasadena, California. Membership in the American Institute of Physics and the American Association for the Advancement of Science.

Following are some interesting excerpts from those interviews:

Question: What are some of the paradoxical aspects of quantum physics—I think Einstein called it "spooky action"—what are some of the anomalies that are causing all these questions and theories involving consciousness?

> **Hugh Ross**: Ultimately, it is founded on the Heisenberg uncertainty principle where, because of that uncertainty, the human observer is not able to get access to the causality phenomena…. Because the causality is hidden from view, a number of people think they are free to speculate about weird or spooky things about what is happening on the level of cause and effect.

> **Marj Hartman**: I should point out that this does not mean that there are hidden variables that should be included in the theory—that is not what we are talking about.

Question: Does this have to do with the fact that an electron can have both wave and particle properties, and whatever you test for seems to be what you find?

> **Erica Carlson**: There is wave/particle duality. That means that sometimes when you are testing these things they appear to have wave properties and sometimes when you are testing them, they appear to have particle properties. I was reading in the Feynman Lectures recently—Richard Feynman has some great explanations of these things…and he had a great statement where he said basically that we gave up trying to decide whether it was a particle or a wave and we decided it is kind of both/and. Really, whatever is going on at that very small level, where quantum mechanics plays in, you do

see some particle-like properties and some wave-like properties and they are both there.

Question: My understanding of the claims made by some wanting to give cosmic or spiritual interpretations of this is that whatever the scientists are looking for is what they find. Thus, the conclusion that they draw is that the perception [or thought] creates the reality. The [element] actually changes depending on what the scientist is thinking.

Erica Carlson: Well, there is a phrase in quantum mechanics literature called "observer determines reality." If you haven't had all of the mathematical background behind what that means, then certainly that statement is open to misinterpretation. So let me give you an analogy as to what that means....

Set a coin spinning on the table and, while the coin is spinning, it is neither heads nor tails—because it is spinning. If you want to find out if it is heads or tails, you will have to change it to find that out. So in a sense, it did not have a property of either heads or tails beforehand but it does have a probability of being heads or tails. When I knock it down and flatten it on the table, it has a 50 percent chance of being either.

The analogy here is...when you take a measurement of something in quantum mechanics, you do change the state (most of the time) but you don't have any control [over] what pops up. That is where the fallacy often comes in. Just like the spinning coin, I do not have any control [over] whether it pops up heads or tails—but there is a 50 percent chance it will do one or the other. I do control the fact that it will go into one of those states but I don't control which one.... It is very much like rolling the dice and you don't know what answer it will be.

Hugh Ross: The bottom line again is that the causality is hidden from view and, therefore, people are speculating upon all kinds of nonsense about that causality, including this idea that somehow we human beings are affecting the cause-and-effect reaction. One of the principles we do see in quantum mechanics is that the human observer or the human instruments we use are simply irrelevant to the causality. The problem here is that by trying to observe the system we wind up disturbing it—very dramatically....

There is a possibility of deception here in the thinking that we are somehow controlling the whole thing and that we are somehow the creator of all this. Particularly in the entropic principle—some really wild speculations going on that, in effect, deify the human observer....

Quantum mechanics told us that there were fundamental limitations to the degree that we could take our level of investigation in instrumental measurement. So it turns out that we are weaker in our capacity to check out causality than we thought before we discovered quantum mechanics. That is my main complaint about these documentaries and books [is that] they are trying to claim the very opposite of what quantum principles demonstrate.

Marj Hartman: Even Niels Bohr, who is the father of the Copenhagen interpretation [of quantum mechanics] said that it is certainly not possible for the observer to influence the events, which may appear under the conditions that he has arranged. Our possibilities of handling the measuring instruments allow us only to make a choice between the different complementary types of phenomena that you want to study. In other words, the observer determines what you want to study but beyond that, you don't have any effect.

They keep saying, "Our minds are connected to everything" and "We are energy, we influence the universe by our consciousness." If an experimenter tries to influence his experiment using only his consciousness and no measuring instrument, he will not get any results.

Erica Carlson: That is absolutely correct.... Can our thoughts affect things? That probably goes back to a misunderstanding of that phrase "observer determines reality."...but what do we mean by *observer* in quantum mechanics? It doesn't have anything to do with consciousness. The observer that is talked about in a quantum mechanical sense is actually a measurement device. So it doesn't need any consciousness whatsoever. It has nothing to do with your consciousness or mine. It's just not linked.

Question: About quantum entanglement—can you explain what Einstein meant when he talked about "spooky action at a distance"? What was that all about?

Robert Park: Well, you're getting right to the heart of it. Let me describe what it is we don't understand, and that is quantum entanglement. We do know that an electron, in addition to being a particle...it has a quality that we call spin, which is oriented in a particular direction, so we can align the spins of electrons. The total is always zero, and that for every spin-up you are going to have a spin-down. Now, somehow those electrons remember their state so if those two electrons come back in contact, they know what they are supposed to be. Now, let me give you an analogy of this.

It may not be quite as profound as it seems.... Here is an analogy. Suppose that I have a red marble and a black marble. What I am going to do is put each of them in a box, two separate boxes that look identical, and now I am going to shuffle them so that nobody knows which is in which box. I am going to climb in a rocket ship and take one of those boxes with me, and a colleague is going to get in another rocket ship and go in the opposite direction. We are going to head out across the universe as far as we can go. We will both carry a clock with us. At some agreeable time, we will open our boxes. The minute I open my box, I know what he is seeing in his box, of course, despite the fact that he is halfway across the universe, of course, but no information is passed. It is only that that entanglement, when we put the two marbles in the boxes, that entanglement is still there....

Question: I think that what I believe Dr. Wolf or some of the scientists on *What the Bleep!?*—their point is if you change the properties of one, it instantly changes the properties of the other even if it is light years away.

[They allege that this proves that information is traveling at infinite speed (which is impossible) or that in reality, the distance between them is not real. From this, they argue that quantum entanglement proves that the reality of distance or space is actually an illusion. Because everything in the universe was entangled at the moment of the big bang, everything in the universe is actually still touching. "Space is just a construct that gives the illusion that there are separate objects."[14] All is one.]

> **Robert Park**: And no, it doesn't mean that you change the properties of the other; it just means that you know what the properties are of the other even though you haven't measured it.

Question: So in quantum entanglement no information is being transmitted at all, there is not actually any change taking place instantaneously?

> **Robert Park**: There is not change taking place.

Question: Okay, that helps a lot. And of course, I think then maybe it is misrepresenting.

> **Robert Park**: It is misstating it.

Question: So, it misstates the principle and then there is a [faulty] conclusion that is drawn that shows that all things are interconnected?

> **Robert Park**: Yes.

Question: I have Jack Canfield, Rhonda Byrne, and several people in *The Secret* saying that it has actually now been scientifically proven that everything is really energy—implying, if not stating, that matter doesn't exist or is somehow illusionary.

> **Hugh Ross**: In looking at this material, I think a fundamental fallacy is that they are trying to come up with some way to violate the first law of thermodynamics (that energy can neither be created nor

destroyed within the universe). They are trying to get something for nothing. In other words, if I just have these certain thoughts, that are energy states in my mind, that somehow I can generate a much bigger energy effect outside of my human realm....

Erica Carlson: To say that everything is really energy is a very odd statement. I think they must be just misunderstanding $E=mc^2$. You can convert matter into energy and you can convert energy into matter. The energy scales of that, however, are so high—that is what nuclear reactors do. They are accessing part of that matter and converting those things into energy at the nuclear level. You don't want to do this with your body. That is way too high of an energy scale.

So if you would convert all of the matter in me into energy, it would be a lot of energy but it is not the kind of energy that you can access. That doesn't mean, either, that I am energy. My physical body is made up of matter at the moment. It has a mass. You could convert it to energy but it is not energy at the moment....

There is another challenge I would like to put forth to these people. If they think they can use their minds to control things, why don't they go solve the problem of AIDS orphans in Africa or why don't they provide clean drinking water to all the poverty-stricken areas of the world?

Question: When Drs. Hagelin and Wolf say that quantum physics proves that perception creates reality or the mind interacts with matter, and either manipulates or creates matter, is that the position of the mainstream scientific community?

Robert Park: Absolutely not.

Question: You know Dr. Hagelin?

Robert Park: I know Dr. Hagelin. He was doing fairly good work at the Stanford Linear Accelerator [Center] when he underwent some sort of a personal crisis, disappeared from sight for I think almost a year. He reemerged as the head of the physics department at the Maharishi University, and at that point, he had somehow fallen under the spell of the Maharishi and now began to believe all of these mysterious things.

In fact, the last time I saw Hagelin, he came to Washington during the problems in Kosovo and he came to see Madeleine Albright to try to get money to recruit a large coterie—I think something like 1,000 trained transcendental meditators. They were going to go to Kosovo and meditate in unison, spreading a peace shield over Kosovo, and it would solve all the problems.

Question: Which I guess corresponds to that theory of his that visualization or meditation or concentration, mental activity…

Robert Park: Corresponds to that theory, but not to any theory that any scientist knows anything about. Well, Madeleine Albright turned him down. I thought that was a terrible mistake.

Question: On whose part?

Robert Park: I thought it probably would have ended the war because they would have been laughing too hard to fight! In fact, at that time he came to the National Press Club, where I have an office, and [he] actually gave a demonstration of Transcendental Meditation in which the best-trained transcendental meditators are supposedly able to levitate. So he gave us a demonstration of levitation.

Hugh Ross: That is a fundamental teaching in TM, that if you are a good enough meditator, you can levitate your body and go wherever you want.

Robert Park: He brought out a dozen fit young guys, they looked very fit, and spread mattresses right there on the floor in the National Press building and they assumed the lotus position, and began meditating. We were all cautioned that we should be quiet while they were meditating so as not to disturb their meditation. After what seemed a very long time, but was probably a couple of minutes, one of them suddenly levitated. Well, he didn't exactly float out the door; he popped up and thumped right back down on the mattress. And then another one popped up; and when I say popped up, maybe an inch.

Question: Okay, let me ask, was it hovering or hopping?

Robert Park: Well, he looked, he managed to maintain the lotus position and I couldn't testify whether he followed a parabolic trajectory, but I would bet on it, but what he was doing quite clearly was constricting his sphincter muscles, and there is a long story behind that. But at any rate, I admire their athleticism. They have trained many, many hours to be able to pop themselves up maybe an inch. They have published loads of photographs taken by cameras that, of course, catch them at the top and it looks like they are just hovering.

Question: Did you witness anything that violated the known laws of physics or gravity?

Robert Park: Not a thing. As a matter of fact, after just a few minutes of this, after each hop, these guys would be panting heavily and then they would sum up enough energy to hop again. It looked like corn popping after a while. I'm telling you this would have stopped any warfare, the sight of 1,000, 10,000, or however many transcendental meditators it was going to take—that would have ended it. This was the funniest thing I have ever seen.

Now Hagelin…conducted an experiment here in Washington to create serenity here in Washington by bringing transcendental meditators. He brought in 4,000 transcendental meditators from around the country and they spent two weeks in Washington, again meditating in unison to try to spread a peace shield over Washington. The result was that the murder rate in Washington soared to an all-time high. It was the wildest two weeks you've ever seen. Each Monday the *Washington Post* would publish the fatalities over the weekend of murder and mayhem, and yet he continues to refer to the success of that experiment, refers to it over and over. He made runs for the presidency of the United States; he made a great point of this and how he was going to stop crime all over the country with his meditation. I don't think the meditation caused the violence, but it certainly didn't end it.

Question: In *The Secret,* Dr. Hagelin states that the universe actually emerges from thought.

> *Quantum mechanics confirms it. Quantum cosmology confirms it. That the Universe essentially emerges from thought and that all of this matter around us is just pre-cipitated thought. Ultimately we are the source of the Universe, and when we understand that power directly by experience, we can start to exercise our authority and begin to achieve more and more. Create anything. Know anything, from within the field from our own conscious-ness, which ultimately is Universal consciousness that runs the Universe.*[15]
>
> JOHN HAGELIN

Robert Park: Well that's wonderful; I've got a few things I'd like for him to create! What in the world is he talking about? I have absolutely no idea.

Erica Carlson: That must be a real misunderstanding of the "observer determines reality" phrase. Consciousness actually doesn't play into it. He is wrong on that count that thought has anything to do with it at all. Also, quantum mechanics still has to obey cause and effect. So to postulate that people somehow created the universe by observing it would have to be wrong on two counts. [It is wrong] for thinking that consciousness has anything to do with the quantum mechanical observation—it doesn't, and for thinking that you can violate cause and effect.

Question: So there is nothing in your understanding of physics and quantum physics, there is nothing that Dr. Hagelin could be drawing on and maybe have a faulty conclusion—you don't even know the premise that he is even starting with on this?

Robert Park: I have no idea what this guy is talking about....

ARE THE SCIENTIFIC CLAIMS VALID?

Perhaps for the sake of fair evaluation, the issues surrounding the Maharishi should be set aside for the time being. Yogic flying and creating world peace through TM are rather bizarre concepts for traditional scientists. These are theories of the Maharishi and Dr. Hagelin, however, and not those put forth directly by Rhonda Byrne.

The real questions here do not pertain to Transcendental Meditation or the academic credentials and beliefs of the experts. The real questions raised by *The Secret* do not have to do with the theories behind the scientific statements. The important questions here relate to the *scientific claims themselves.*

- *Are any of the scientific claims valid?*
- *Can the science behind* The Secret *be verified in the lab?*
- *What does the scientific community in general think of the secret science?*

These questions will be best answered by examining some of the scientific claims themselves and breaking down the subatomic thinking.

SUBATOMIC THINKING

I never studied science or physics at school, and yet when I read complex books on quantum physics I understood them perfectly because I wanted to understand them. The study of quantum physics helped me to have a deeper understanding of The Secret, on an energetic level. For many people, their belief is strengthened when they see the perfect correlation between the knowledge of The Secret and the theories of new science.[1]

RHONDA BYRNE, AUTHOR OF *THE SECRET*

I would have to give Rhonda Byrne the grade of F.[2]

ERICA CARLSON, PH.D., ASSISTANT PROFESSOR OF
PHYSICS, PURDUE UNIVERSITY

Quantum physics is a branch of theoretical physics that measures and studies the structure and behavior of atoms and subatomic particles. The experts featured in *The Secret* testify that quantum physics and other "new science" are "in total harmony with" and verify the Law of Attraction.

In the previous chapters, we discussed the background and beliefs of some of the experts. We also addressed some of the underlying theories put forth in *The Secret* and *What the Bleep!?*

SCIENTISTS SPEAK OUT ABOUT THE SCIENTIFIC CLAIMS

In this chapter, we would like to go beyond the theories and examine some of the claims themselves—on their own merits. We have asked our same panel of scientists and researchers, introduced in the previous chapter, to address some of the scientific statements made in *The Secret*.

> *Let me explain how you are the most powerful transmission tower in the Universe. In simple terms, all energy vibrates at a frequency. Being energy, you also vibrate at a frequency, and what determines your frequency at any time is whatever you are thinking and feeling. All the things you want are made of energy, and they are vibrating too.* Everything *is energy.*
>
> *Here is the "wow" factor. When you think about what you want, and you emit that frequency, you cause the energy of what you want to vibrate at that frequency and you bring it to You! As you focus on what you want, you are changing the vibration of the atoms of that thing, and you are causing it to vibrate to You. The reason you are the most powerful transmission tower in the Universe is because you have been given the power to focus your energy through your thoughts and alter the vibrations of*

> *what you are focused on, which then magnetically draws*
> *it to you.*[3]
>
> RHONDA BYRNE

Erica Carlson: This quote from Rhonda Byrne is so wrong I don't know where to start with it. She says, "Being energy, you also vibrate at a frequency...," but you are not energy. She says if you focus on what you want, you change the vibration of the atoms. That is just off. Your thoughts are not interacting with quantum mechanics.

Hugh Ross: She says, "I read complex books on quantum physics I understood them perfectly." This is selective reading. I see this all across the religious front. People will look at something and they will mark out what they want to hear and they will let the rest go. I would agree with Erica. Just reading this, where do you begin in critiquing it? It is just so absurd in terms of its response to fundamental physics.... She is not understanding what she is reading.

Erica Carlson: That is absolutely right, she is not understanding what she is reading.

Hugh Ross: Even for the Ph.D.s making these claims in *The Secret* you want to say, "I hear what you are saying about quantum mechanics, but how defensible are your statements before an audience where everyone in the audience has a Ph.D. in physics? Have you ever made these kinds of claims at UCLA or Caltech, or at Harvard?"

Marj Hartman: It all goes back to the fact that on the quantum level, you can't measure without interfering. From that, they [misunderstand the statement] "the observer determines reality." Even Werner Heisenberg,[4] who formulated the uncertainty principle, said that observations of quantum events apply to the physical—not psychical—act of observation. He said that quantum theory does not introduce the mind of the physicist as part of the atomic event.

Erica Carlson: One of the fallacies that I have seen in *The Secret* is that consciousness somehow affects quantum mechanical outcomes, and that is completely false. Consciousness does not play into these things at all. A measuring apparatus is what we mean by "observer" in quantum mechanics. There is no consciousness there. Also, this idea that you can control outcomes is false....

> *The law of attraction is the law of creation. Quantum physicists tell us that the entire Universe emerged from thought! You create your life through your thoughts and the law of attraction, and every single person does the same.... When you become aware of this great law, then you become aware of how incredibly powerful you are, to be able to THINK your life into existence.*[5]
>
> RHONDA BYRNE

Robert Park: From thought? Is she suggesting that nothing happened until people were around to think? That sort of defies everything we know. That is so wacky it is indescribable. That might be very comforting to people, and people like to believe comforting things. But it just has absolutely no basis in reality.

> *Time is just an illusion. Einstein told us that. If this is the first time you have heard it, you may find it a hard concept to get your head around, because you see every-thing happening—one thing after the other. What quantum physicists and Einstein tell us is that everything is happening simultaneously. If you can understand that there is no time, and accept that concept, then you will see that whatever you want in the future already exists. If everything is happening at the one time, then the parallel version of you with what you want already exists.*[6]
>
> RHONDA BYRNE

Robert Park: Einstein never said that time was an illusion.

Erica Carlson: [This is] another fallacy...that time is not a real thing.

That is false. Every formulation of quantum mechanics had to preserve "causality"—the cause needs to precede the effect. That is in every theory of quantum mechanics and that is in Einstein's theory of special relativity.

Robert Park: [Einstein's theory pertains to] the fact that clocks can run at a different rate depending on your relative motion. All that Einstein said [was] that he was able to predict how much a clock would be slowed down by moving at a high speed. [She is making] a total leap; it has nothing to do with time being an illusion.

> *I want to go back to that initial thought that you were telling us about how you send out, your thoughts go out into the universe and there's a vibration. You first have to explain that we really are all just energy, we are all just energy, where all can you explain that?*
>
> OPRAH WINFREY

> *Basically everything is energy. If you go to quantum physics we realize everything is energy and what controls the flow of energy is thought and feeling; it's a vibration.... And all of a sudden the people, the resources, the ideas, the strategies, start appearing in your life and become magnetized toward you.[7]*
>
> JACK CANFIELD

Robert Park: It is so confused.... There is this tiny grain of truth behind all of it, that there are vibrations, but you don't attract them back to you.... We certainly do have attractive forces in the universe [but] the idea that like attracts like is contradicted constantly. What attracts is opposites, negative attracts positive, if you are talking about electro-magnetic attraction.

> *I'm talking to you from a deeper, basic understanding. Quantum physics really begins to point to this discovery. It*

> *says that you can't have a Universe without mind entering into it, and that the mind is actually shaping the very thing that is being perceived.*[8]
>
> FRED ALAN WOLF, QUANTUM PHYSICIST FEATURED IN
> *WHAT THE BLEEP!?* AND *THE SECRET*

Robert Park: They are playing the pseudoscience game. They are using scientific terminology to explain things that are not scientific....

QUANTUM MEDICINE?

If the general public is given mistaken information in the name of quantum physics, this causes problems on a number of levels. A much more serious crisis results when such information is given to the gravely ill as a form of medical advice.

- *Does the secret cure cancer?*

- *Does seeing overweight people actually create obesity?*

- *Do treating and paying attention to a disease actually cause it to exist?*

We will discuss the hidden cause of all illness and the potential source of total wellness as we explore the promises behind secret medicine.

9

SECRET MEDICINE

I was diagnosed with breast cancer. I truly believed in my heart, with my strong faith, that I was already healed.

Each day I would say, "Thank you for my healing." On and on and on I went, "Thank you for my healing." I believed in my heart I was healed. I saw myself as if cancer was never in my body.[1]

CATHY GOODMAN, CANCER SURVIVOR
FEATURED IN *THE SECRET*

According to *The Secret,* the mysterious and secret Law of Attraction not only creates all poverty and riches, it is also the underlying cause of all illness and wellness.

The Secret preaches a powerful and controversial theory concerning sickness and disease. It is the same theory once whispered by the early followers of some controversial sects who had their beginnings in small religious gatherings over a century ago.

They had become enlightened. They discovered that, on some fundamental level, sickness and disease are not real. They are illusions. The symptoms of illness are mere "manifestations" of the illusions. They are simply a by-product of wrong thinking.

Cancer, diabetes, AIDS, heart disease, and high blood pressure are actually products of our imaginations. Thinking thoughts of wellness and perfect health causes one to "demonstrate over" the illusion—illusions of pain, sickness, and even death. Byrne agrees.

THE SECRET DIET

Even obesity and weight loss have been inexorably connected to the principles of *The Secret.* According to Byrne, neither food, calories, fat, exercise, metabolism, nor physiology have anything to do with how much you weigh.

You have tried Atkins, South Beach, Weight Watchers, and Nutrisystem. None of them worked? Now you know why.

According to the Law of Attraction, thinking about weight loss actually attracts more weight. Remember that the Universe does not understand words such as *don't, not,* and *no.*[2] Therefore, when you think "weight *loss,*" the universe only hears the first part, "weight," and responds, "Your wish is my command."

> *The most common thought that people hold, and I held it too, is that food was responsible for my weight gain. That*

is a belief that does not serve you, and in my mind now it is complete balderdash! Food is not responsible for putting on weight. It is your thought that food is responsible for putting on weight that actually has food put on weight. Remember, thoughts are primary cause of everything, and the rest is effects from those thoughts. Think perfect thoughts and the result must be perfect weight.[3]

RHONDA BYRNE

For the obese, Byrne recommends scrapping the diet. Instead of an exercise program or a diet, Byrne recommends imagining yourself at the perfect weight and finding a picture of yourself at that perfect weight to look at often. You must "pretend" and "make believe" that you are the perfect weight and (this part is important) don't weigh yourself. "Do not contradict what you have asked for with your thoughts, words, and actions." If you must weigh yourself, "Write out your perfect weight and place it over the readout of your scale."[4]

According to the Law of Attraction, looking at overweight people is what causes a person to attract pounds. "If you see people who are overweight, do not observe them, but immediately switch your mind to the picture of you in your perfect body and *feel* it."[5]

If you're a woman trying to lose weight, you had your choice of two pieces of advice last week. One, from the American Heart Association, was to eat more vegetables and exercise an hour a day. The other was from a woman named Rhonda Byrne...Byrne's recommendation was to avoid looking at fat people.... So if you're having trouble giving up ice cream, maybe you could just cut back on "The Sopranos" instead.[6]

JERRY ADLER, *NEWSWEEK*

When it comes to illness and disease, the advice gets even more coun-terintuitive—if that is possible. The cure for every illness and disease is proper thinking. "Illness cannot exist in a body that has harmonious thoughts."[7]

LAUGHTER REALLY *IS* THE BEST MEDICINE?

The Secret cites three major examples of mental healing—Morris Goodman, "the Miracle Man," who survived a near-fatal plane crash; his wife, Cathy Goodman, who survived breast cancer; and Norman Cousins, who was healed of an unnamed "incurable" disease that was thought to be fatal.

Cousins decided to cure himself, so he prescribed 90 days of a heavy dose of funny movies that helped him "laugh, laugh, laugh."[8] His doctors called his recuperation a miracle. He attributes the recovery to the laughter, which he says released all negativity—and with it the disease. His story inspired Cathy Goodman to shun radiation and chemotherapy for laughter. The laughter was in alignment with the Law of Attraction.

> *One of the things I did to heal myself was to watch very funny movies. That's all we would do was just laugh, laugh, and laugh. We couldn't afford to put any stress in my life, because we knew stress was one of the worst things you can do while you're trying to heal yourself.*
>
> *From the time I was diagnosed to the time I was healed was approximately three months. And that's without any radiation or chemotherapy.*[9]
>
> CATHY GOODMAN

Michael Bernard Beckwith reports, "I've seen kidneys regenerated. I've seen cancer dissolved. I've seen eyesight improve and come back."[10] According to *The Secret*, there is no disease that is incurable. In fact, incurable really means *curable from within.*[11]

The Law of Attraction even defeats the most universal disease of all—aging. Like other physical disabilities and disease, aging is an illusion.

> *You can see that beliefs about aging are all in our minds. Science explains that we have a brand new body in a very short time. Aging is limited thinking, so release those thoughts from your consciousness and know that your body is only months old, no matter how many birthdays you have chalked up in your mind. For your next birthday, do yourself a favor and celebrate it as your first birthday! Don't cover your cake with sixty candles, unless you want to summon aging to you. Unfortunately, Western society has become fixated on age, and in reality there is no such thing.*[12]
>
> RHONDA BYRNE

GETTING A MEDICAL PERSPECTIVE

Is there data or research to back up the promises in *The Secret*? Could the answer to cancer, heart disease, and aging really be as simple as changing one's mind? Are all diseases really just psychosomatic?

To provide some perspective concerning the connection between the mind and disease we conducted an interview[13] with Dr. Richard Sloan, professor of behavioral medicine (in psychiatry) at the New York Presbyterian Hospital at the Columbia University Medical Center. Sloan also serves as chief of the division of behavioral medicine at New York State Psychiatric Institute.

Question: Oprah has generated immense interest in Rhonda Byrne's testimony and her claim that this is a secret. I see that your expertise is in cognitive behavioral science (CBS).... Would you be willing to respond to some of the claims?

Richard Sloan: Yes, of course, certainly.

Question: [In the book *The Secret,* a breast cancer patient, Cathy Goodman, provides a testimonial. Using some of the principles of the Law of Attraction, she decided to forego radiation and chemotherapy and focus on reducing stress. She claims that she was able to heal herself by watching funny movies helping her to eliminate stress through laughter.] She says that she was miraculously healed in three months.

In your experience in CBS, does the mind have the power to effect healing? If so, in what way?

> **Richard Sloan**: I would rather go at it from a different perspective. There are clearly psychological characteristics that influence certain diseases. For instance, depression is widely recognized to increase the risk of heart disease. There is no evidence, that I know, of a role that psychological factors play in cancer. In fact, almost all of the studies are negative.

Question: Is creating an environment for cancer to develop and/or in reversing that [possible]?

> **Richard Sloan**: Yes, but even expressing it that way does not address Goodman's ridiculous claims. Because people have looked at whether personality characteristics—like depression, for example, or hostility or anxiety—may play a role in development of disease or exacerbation of disease and in some disease, like heart disease, the answer is yes. In other diseases, like cancer, the answer appears to be no.
>
> That is not the same thing as saying that basically you can whistle a happy tune as Jiminy Cricket did fifty years ago [in Walt Disney's *Pinocchio*] and cause your disease to disappear. Those are two very different things.
>
> This woman's cancer may have disappeared. She may never have had cancer to begin with. It may have been a bad diagnosis. It may have been misreading of a diagnostic test or it could in fact have disappeared. There are things we do not understand in medicine.

But, there is nothing that we know of in the real world that can account for any of the claims in this book [*The Secret*], whether they are medically related or otherwise. The universe is not a kind of cosmic vending machine in which we deposit thought and then pull the goodies out of the tray.

Question: That is exactly what they are claiming, a universal catalog...

Richard Sloan: All you have to do is believe hard enough, think hard enough. Of course, if you don't succeed, you are disparaged because you didn't believe or think hard enough. You didn't think the right thoughts.

Question: This is rampant teaching [also] within the health-and-prosperity churches?

Richard Sloan: Yes.

Question: That if you fail to "manifest" that which you have been focusing on, praying for, then there is a problem with you?

Richard Sloan: That is right. There is a problem with you. That is precisely the point.

Question: [Are] you just adding to the misery of the patient?

Richard Sloan: Right, it is bad enough that he is sick but to add to that the burden of some supposed failure is just really cruel....

Question: [Are] your expertise and research more in the area of cardiac health and cognitive behavior affecting the heart?

Richard Sloan: Yes.

Question: You made the statement earlier that there is no evidence that cancer is affected in any way by emotions.

Richard Sloan: Right.

Question: Well, I will use myself. I have had two heart attacks. I have a significant amount of scar tissue along the bottom of my right ventricle. So, according to *The Secret,* I should be able to totally repair my heart?

Richard Sloan: It certainly would seem that way.

Question: It would seem that way. Clinically, in all of the years you have been dealing with this, have you seen anyone, just through mental healing exercises, any evidence, that that has brought them back to full health?

> **Richard Sloan**: No, I don't think so. As I said before, there are things we don't understand in medicine. For every thousand people or ten thousand people, some may get better on their own for reasons we don't fully understand. But, you cannot look at a single case and make claims that it characterizes the general response. It is a single isolated case. Ninety-nine times out of a hundred a person who is sick with a certain disease is going to remain sick until there is some sort of a medical intervention or unless it is a disease that is self-limiting, like a cold. You don't have a cold forever.

[In discussing the controversial and similar teachings of the health and wealth gospel of modern-day Word Faith preachers, Christian researcher Rob Bowman draws a similar conclusion: "Think of it this way. Suppose thirty thousand people pack a convention center to hear Benny Hinn. Many of these people will come in hope of obtaining healing. Let us suppose for the sake of illustration that 1 percent of the attendees have serious diseases or infirmities from which they want relief. (The number is presumably higher.) Out of those three hundred people, if nothing at all happens out of the ordinary, a good many of them will get better. For example, some people with cancer will have it go into remission. The point is that out of that crowd of thirty thousand, what would really be surprising would be if no one left feeling significantly better."][14]

Question: What would you like...the public [to know concerning this]?

> **Richard Sloan**: Well, you know there are some other issues I imagine you will consider—the sort of social implications of this because *The Secret* applies not only to matters of health, and medicine, but

to social roles and the accumulation of wealth. Presumably, all you need to do is think about it and untold fortunes will come your way. That BMW is just waiting for you [and] that Rolex watch.

So what does it say to people who are stuck in poverty? So what does it say to people who are stuck in Katrina-decimated New Orleans? What does it say to the people who were in the World Trade Center?

The broader concern is that it encourages an incredible kind of passivity. You don't actually have to do anything. You don't have to work for something. You just have to think it, and it will come your way.

Well, some other thoughts, some background—this book appears with some regularity about every five years or so. It just changes names. Ten years ago it was *The Celestine Prophecy*. Five years ago it was something else. They keep appearing. They say the same thing. They make claims that the universe is designed to deliver precisely whatever you want if only you think it properly. So, it is nothing new at all. The astonishing thing is that every five years it comes out and jumps to the top of the best-seller list.

Question: Especially when Oprah Winfrey pushes it and says this is how she has lived her life.

Richard Sloan: [That is] right, and you know Oprah has actually done a lot to empower women in this country but this is a real disservice.

Question: People that have tremendous public influence need to be extra careful.

Richard Sloan: They have an extraordinary degree of responsibility and they have to exercise it carefully.

NO LAUGHING MATTER

Great influence calls for great responsibility. This is true whether one influences millions through a daily television program or through a best-selling book.

Dr. Sloan reminds us of a significant unintended outcome from the Law of Attraction. If all that is unpleasant, bad, or evil is a product of wrong thinking, then all your pain, suffering, and tragedy is *your* fault, and *Secret* teacher Joe Vitale has every right to get in your face and tell you that you *did* attract the cancer, the car accident,[15] or for that matter, the Holocaust.

This also means that when you practice the Law of Attraction, you must be very creative with the truth. It encourages a "fake it till you make it" bravado.

How are you feeling? Well, do you want the truth, or a positive affirmation? If I tell you the truth, it creates the reality of how bad I feel. So I guess I feel fine. No, I feel perfect—in every way.

Are you broke? Let's see, I must be very careful how I answer that question because the universe is listening. Umm, I have more money than Bill Gates.

The Law of Attraction is also not falsifiable—at least in verbal testimony. If someone testifies that an aspect of *The Secret* is not working, the negative thought and word itself creates the negative outcome. Thus, the Law of Attraction is proven true after all.

This places people in a double bind.[16] They must either falsely confess that all is well and the Law of Attraction is working, or tell the truth and manifest their woes. If they are honest, then their "negative confession" is charged with creating the very problem they are reporting. Either way, all of their financial or medical problems are totally their fault for not practicing the Law of Attraction correctly.[17]

This kind of thinking is fraught with problems and is harmful enough when applied to new watches or a sports car. It is all the more problematic when applied to medical conditions.

Teaching someone how to use *The Secret* to attract luxury items is different than teaching them how to use it to manifest medical cures. While the same Law of Attraction is employed, failed outcomes have far more serious consequences with the latter.

- *Is there a responsibility or even a liability for dispensing questionable medical advice?*

- *Have people actually stopped life-saving medical treatment after being prescribed the Law of Attraction?*

- *Could this secret cost you your life?*

To discover the answers, we must first come face-to-face with the secret consequences.

SECRET CONSEQUENCES

The question frequently asked is, "When a person has manifested a disease in the body temple or some kind of discomfort in their life, can it be turned around through the power of 'right' thinking?"

And the answer is absolutely, yes.[1]

MICHAEL BERNARD BECKWITH, THE AGAPE INTERNATIONAL SPIRITUAL CENTER, FEATURED IN *THE SECRET*

You don't have to fight to get rid of a disease. Just the simple process of letting go of negative thoughts will allow your natural state of health to emerge within you. And your body will heal itself.[2]

RHONDA BYRNE, AUTHOR OF *THE SECRET*

There can be little doubt that Rhonda Byrne believes in *The Secret*. She testifies to having used the Law of Attraction to manifest her perfect weight, throw away her reading glasses, suspend the aging process, and "banished every bit of stiffness and lack of agility right out...overnight."[3]

Her millions of readers attempting to follow in her footsteps may not be so adept. Countless readers of *The Secret* are fighting chronic illness and potentially terminal disease. Are they now going to be reluctant to talk with their doctors about the disease lest they give "energy" to the illness by thinking about it?

> *Disease is held in the body by thought, by observation of the illness, and by the attention given to the illness. If you are feeling a little unwell, don't talk about it—unless you want more of it. If you listen to people talk about their illness, you add energy to theirs. Instead, change the conversation to good things, and give powerful thoughts to seeing those people in health.*[4]
>
> RHONDA BYRNE

If disease is held in the body by thinking about it, then every time we take medicine we are acknowledging our need and thinking about the disease. If listening to people talk about their disease also causes sickness, then virtually any conversation with your doctor is doubly harmful. Can someone acknowledge, discuss, and receive traditional medical treatment while still being true to the Law of Attraction?

Fortunately, not all the teachers in *The Secret* are as zealous as Byrne. Dr. John Demartini advises readers to continue taking medicine in those acute cases that could result in death.[5] Likewise, in his interview on *Nightline*, Bob Proctor rather reluctantly admitted if it had been his decision, *The Secret* would not have included Cathy Goodman's testimony about rejecting chemotherapy and radiation treatments. He said he personally would receive any treatment his doctor prescribed.[6]

Hopefully, most fans of *The Secret* will also think twice before using it as a cancer cure. Conceivably most of Byrne's readers will experiment with the Law of Attraction only for personal gain. Perhaps they will just try to win the lottery, manifest some jewelry, or attract a new home. When it doesn't work, they won't have lost much. Most will just be disappointed. But isn't *The Secret* a law, like gravity, that always works?

Follow the Money

No, the Law of Attraction does not always work, and money might be a good example. While an "attitude of gratitude" and a positive outlook are good and helpful, good thoughts are not magic. They do not create things out of nothing. A financial example may be helpful.

At some time or another, most everyone has accidentally overdrawn their checking account. It's called bouncing a check. Now the interesting thing here is that most of those times, the people were absolutely positive that they had enough money in their account to cover that check. In fact, everyone involved in the transaction was sending out good vibrations.

What happened to the Law of Attraction? Let's play "follow the money."

1. You wrote the check having positive thoughts. You knew the check was good, so you were sending out positive energy.

2. The cashier who took your check was very affirming and received your check with a spirit of faith and gratitude.

3. When the cashier deposited your check, the bank teller was equally confident it would clear. Everyone was smiling and the universe was happy.

Everything was fine until the bank's computers became involved. They were not human. They were not visualizing debt, thinking bad thoughts, or sending any negative vibrations. They were just doing the math.

Despite all the positive attitudes and good feelings on the part of every human involved along the way, there was a greater reality in play. That reality is called your available balance. Eventually your bank sends you a notice of enlightenment, alerting you to this problem that never even crossed your mind—or anyone else's.

What was the cost of your enlightenment? A mere $22.50 service charge. That is a rather small price to pay for such an important lesson about the nature of the universe.

THE BANK VS. THE HOSPITAL

If you are making life-and-death medical decisions using the principles of *The Secret*, the stakes become much higher. What happens when someone takes the Law of Attraction from the bank to the hospital?

Some might ask, "But would reasonable people actually make critical healthcare choices based on the advice of channeled beings? Would well-educated people risk their lives to test the theory that, with enough faith, our minds can heal us?" The answer to these questions is yes, and in some cases, it is fatal.

According to John Gorenfeld of *Salon*, JZ Knight's AIDS-stricken husband Jeffrey rejected modern medical treatment based on medical advice given by Ramtha (JZ Knight). Instead of state-of-the-art treatment, he was instructed to heal himself using breathing techniques developed by the Ramtha School of Enlightenment. Jeffrey Knight died.

[Court documents from] Knight's 1992 divorce case with Jeffrey Knight hint that Ramtha is an ancient homophobe, who allegedly declared that AIDS was Mother Nature's way of "getting rid of" homosexuality and told Jeffrey Knight he should reject modern medicine and overcome the disease using the school's breathing techniques, according to court testimony. Tom Szimhart, a "deprogrammer" who testified on behalf of Knight's husband

(who eventually died of the disease) called the Ramtha school a cult with an anti-scientific bent.[7]

JOHN GORENFELD, "THE BLEEP OF FAITH," *SALON*

This is not a new problem. Such healing theories and rejection of medical science can be traced back to those controversial religious sects who had their beginnings in small religious gatherings over a century ago.

For well over 100 years, followers of a brand of religion known as Mind Science have been keeping the faith. Like Byrne, many of them are convinced that disease is an illusion and, with right thinking, they will manifest evidence of perfect health. For some, it is a belief that can lead to death.

Rhonda Byrne not only knows about these nineteenth-century Mind Science religions, she was directly influenced by them.

We find the first clue to this connection in the acknowledgment section of her book, where she recognizes the support and contribution of a man named Charles Fillmore.[8] In 1889, Fillmore and his wife, Myrtle, founded one of the most influential of the Mind Science religions, known as the Unity School of Christianity (or Unity), headquartered in Lee's Summit, Missouri. Their church grew out of their involvement in an obscure nineteenth-century movement known as New Thought.

THE FILLMORES AND MARY BAKER EDDY

Through their studies and associations with other important spiritual innovators of their day, the Fillmores allegedly learned the secret of mental healing. Those studies included more than 40 courses on metaphysics and instruction from Emma Curtis Hopkins, who was extremely prominent in the New Thought movement and a former editor for an earlier Mind Science pioneer, Mary Baker Eddy (1821–1910), founder of the First Church of Christ, Scientist—better known as Christian Science.[9]

Eddy had learned about mental healing from Phineas Parkhurst Quimby (a name often encountered when studying the background and influences of early New Thought religious leaders), who had been a student of the teachings of Franz Anton Mesmer (from which comes the term *mesmerize*). Eddy learned to manifest over the false reality of her own illness and taught her followers that sickness and disease were illusions—doctor visits, medical treatment, and negative thoughts only served to feed the illusion. Eddy's teachings and disciples had a profound impact on many people in the nineteenth century, including the Fillmores.

Myrtle Fillmore, who allegedly suffered from tuberculosis, was awestruck by the phrase, "I am a child of God; therefore, I do not inherit sickness." The resulting change in her thinking, she believed, led to her healing. Eventually the Fillmores earned certification as licensed Christian Science practitioners before breaking ties with Mary Baker Eddy.

Many other Mind Science or New Thought churches sprang up about the same time as the Fillmores'. Like Unity, a number of them, such as the Church of Religious Science, founded by Ernest Holmes, are still active. Byrne's expressed connection to the Fillmores and their teaching may also explain why *The Secret* found its early success in the Mind Science churches and metaphysical bookstores. *Time* magazine reports that before *The Secret* became a mainstream hit at "your local Blockbuster or Barnes & Noble, it [was] selling briskly through new-age bookstores, New Thought churches like Unity and Agape [*Secret* teacher Michael Beckwith's church] and its own Web site www.thesecret.tv."[10]

The TB had flared up again, and the doctors gave [Myrtle Fillmore] six months to live. In desperation she attended, with Charles in tow, a lecture on healing given by E.B. Weeks, a Christian Science practitioner from the Chicago Christian Science school. From this class she learned the now well-known affirmation: "I am a child of God; therefore, I do not inherit sickness." She was able to spend several hours a day in prayer and medititation [sic], working on her heart, lungs and digestive system, and changing the

> *way she thought of her body in general.... The prayer treatment was working, and one by one Myrtle was completely free of her lifelong afflictions.*[11]
>
> UNITY OF KENT, WASHINGTON, "THE BIRTH OF UNITY"

BELIEFS WITH DEADLY CONSEQUENCES

To this day, the followers of Mary Baker Eddy routinely refuse medical treatment, preferring the services of Christian Science practitioners, who instead prescribe a form of prayer and proper thinking. This doctrine has not only led to the premature death of some Christian Scientists, but in some cases has led to the death of their children, as reflected in the following news items:

- *A two-year-old baby girl dies of a treatable lung infection as her mother "follows church guidelines."*[12]

- *In Florida, a family withheld insulin from their diabetic daughter, which resulted in her death.*[13]

- *In 1984, Natalie, an eight-month-old child, died "of complications from a virulent flu-like illness."*[14]

- *In March of 1984, a four-year-old girl "died of meningitis."*[15]

These children of Christian Scientist parents were denied lifesaving medical attention and may have died prematurely from simple-to-treat ailments.

> *Parents who decline traditional medical care in favor of faith healing risk having their children die needlessly, according to a study reported in the April 1998 issue of the journal* Pediatrics. *The study found that most children who died after their parents sought faith healing could have survived if they had been taken for modern medical treatment....*

> *The study was conducted by Dr. Seth M. Asser of the department of pediatrics at the University of California, San Diego, and by Rita Swan of Sioux City, Iowa, a former Christian Scientist. Swan is the founder of the group Children's Healthcare Is a Legal Duty [CHILD, Inc.], begun in 1983 after her 16-month-old son died of meningitis after being treated by Christian Science practitioners.*[16]
>
> EP NEWS, "FAITH HEALING HARMS CHILDREN"

This is not just a hypothetical situation. Belief in mental healing can have significant medical consequences that may mean the difference between life and death.

As we have seen, there are remarkable similarities between the medical theories found in *The Secret* and the doctrines of the Mind Science religions—particularly Christian Science. Now we are also beginning to see a historical link.

- *Are these links coincidental, or are there other solid connections between the Mind Science religions and The Secret?*

- *Is the real science of The Secret found in the theories about atoms, molecules, and vibrations once taught by these long-forgotten ministers and philosophers?*

- *Did these obscure Mind Science teachers warn of some hidden danger or sinister aspect of the Law of Attraction?*

For the answers, we must go back in time 100 years to meet Wallace Wattles.

THE SECRET STARTER

I'd been given a glimpse of a Great Secret—The Secret to life. The glimpse came in a hundred-year-old book, given to me by my daughter Hayley. I began tracing The Secret back through history. I couldn't believe all the people who knew this...Plato, Shakespeare, Newton, Hugo, Beethoven, Lincoln, Emerson, Edison, Einstein.[1]

Gratitude was a fundamental part of the teachings of all the great avatars throughout history. In the book that changed my life, The Science of Getting Rich, *written by Wallace Wattles in 1910, gratitude is its longest chapter.* [2]

RHONDA BYRNE, AUTHOR OF *THE SECRET*

THIS book is pragmatical, not philosophical; a practical manual, not a treatise upon theories. It is intended for the men and women whose most pressing need is for money; who wish to get rich first, and philosophize afterward.[3]

WALLACE WATTLES, OPENING LINES OF
THE SCIENCE OF GETTING RICH

When asked by Oprah why she called it *The Secret,* Rhonda Byrne replied, "We really needed to contain the knowledge in a couple of words. And 'The Secret' is the law of attraction."[4]

Apparently calling the book what she claims it to be, *Law of Attraction,* was too long of a title. We are led to believe that *Secret* conveys the idea of the Law of Attraction better than the words themselves. Of course they don't; it's all about marketing. As Donavin Bennes, a book buyer for Borders who specializes in metaphysics, points out, "It was an incredibly savvy move to call it 'The Secret.' We all want to be in on a secret. But to present it as *the* secret, that was brilliant."[5]

By definition a secret is supposed to be kept to oneself, and not shared. However, there are two facts about secrets that most people can probably agree are true: As Bennes noted, everyone loves to hear or be in on a secret. And once heard, a secret is also difficult not to share with someone else. The marketing machine behind Byrne's DVD and book clearly understands this.

There is a game in which a group of people sit in a circle and someone whispers a secret into the ear of the person seated next to him or her. That person then shares it with the next person, who shares it with the next, and so on until all have heard it. The last person then shares what he or she heard. Very rarely is the final result even close to the original secret that was given.

If playing that game, Byrne would not claim to be the originator of *The Secret,* but a secret-sharer. How close is the message she delivers to the message that was first given? To answer this we must determine who the players are, and which, if any, of them is the secret-starter. Only then can we compare her message with the original one.

THE INFLUENCE OF WALLACE WATTLES

Without question, the channeled entity known as Abraham was important to the development of the original *Secret* DVD and the subsequent remake and book. However, Byrne has consistently credited *The Science of Getting Rich* by Wallace Wattles with initiating the search that would lead to her understanding of the secret. Thus, any examination of *The Secret* must include consideration of Wattles.

There are numerous Internet sites devoted to Wattles, primarily for the purpose of selling his books (which are in the public domain, and some of which have been updated with modern coauthors). Some of these Web sites also share what little is known about his life. Concerning his interest in "things" now being attributed to *The Secret,* many of them point out that "[l]ater in his life he took to studying the various religious beliefs and philosophies of the world including those of Descartes, Spinoza, Leibnitz, Schopenhauer, Hegel, Swedenborg, Emerson, and others. It was through his tireless study and experimentation that he discovered the truth of New Thought principles and put them into practice in his own life." [6]

Shortly after Wattles died, his daughter, Florence, wrote a letter that mentions two facts that obviously influenced the message in his books—his acceptance of a social gospel, and his fear of poverty. She reveals that in 1896 her father met and came under the influence of George D. Herron, an important leader and voice of the socialist movement in America. She also reveals the tremendous impact this meeting had on how her father would live his life. She wrote, "From that day until his death he worked unceasingly to realize the glorious vision of human brotherhood. For years his life was cursed by poverty and the fear of poverty. He was always scheming and planning to get for his family those things which make the abundant life possible." [7] Apparently this "scheming and planning" involved writing, and more importantly, selling numerous publications, such as *The Science of Getting Rich,* which was published in 1910.

Byrne admittedly did draw from this work, yet she clearly states it is not the source for *The Secret,* but the starting point for the journey. And while critics might argue that Wattles's book doesn't even use the term *Law of Attraction,* which is so important to *The Secret,* the concept is certainly contained in lines such as, "The universe desires you to have everything you want to have." [8]

How are these "desires" brought forth? Wattles explains, "Man can form things in his thought, and, by impressing his thought upon formless substance, can cause the thing he thinks about to be created."[9]

> *If you want a sewing machine, for instance, I do not mean to tell you that you are to impress the thought of a sewing machine on Thinking Substance until the machine is formed without hands, in the room where you sit, or elsewhere. But if you want a sewing machine, hold the mental image of it with the most positive certainty that it is being made, or is on its way to you. After once forming the thought, have the most absolute and unquestioning faith that the sewing machine is coming; never think of it, or speak, of it, in any other way than as being sure to arrive. Claim it as already yours. It will be brought to you by the power of the Supreme Intelligence, acting upon the minds of men.*[10]
>
> WALLACE WATTLES

This is certainly what *The Secret* describes as the Law of Attraction when it states, "If you can think about what you want in your mind, and make that your dominant thought, you *will* bring it into your life. Through this most powerful law, your thoughts become the things in your life. Your thoughts become things! Say this over to yourself and let it seep into your consciousness and your awareness. Your thoughts become things!"[11] Perhaps even a sewing machine?

The Emphasis on Getting Rich

However, it is more than just sewing machines on which Wattles and Byrne want you to focus your thoughts. As its title suggests, *The Science of Getting Rich* is about just that—getting rich. Wattles states, "You can make the most of yourself only by getting rich; so it is right and praiseworthy that you should give your first and best thought to the work of acquiring wealth."[12] In fact, Wattles believes this is the divine plan, writing, "It is the desire of God that you should get rich. He wants you to get rich because he can express himself better through you if you have plenty of things to use in giving him expression. He can live more in you if you have unlimited command of the means of life."[13]

But what of *The Secret*? Does Byrne agree with this view that wealth is part of the divine plan? Consider the following: "Now that you know The Secret, when you see someone who is wealthy you will know that that person's predominant thoughts are on wealth and not on scarcity, and that they have *drawn* wealth to them—whether they did it consciously or unconsciously. They focused on thoughts of wealth and the Universe moved people, circumstances, and events to deliver wealth to them."[14]

So the divine/God wants you to be rich so it/he can do even more for you. This message doesn't sound so very different from that of the modern so-called "Christian prosperity" or Word-Faith[15] teachers—such as Kenneth and Gloria Copeland, Charles Capps, Creflo Dollar, et al.—who traverse the country proclaiming that humans are little gods who create their own existence through the power of their words. As Capps once summarized, "God released His faith in words. Man is created in the image of God, therefore man releases his faith in words. Words are the most powerful things in the universe today. Let me say it again, 'The Word of God conceived in the human spirit, formed by the tongue, and spoken out of the mouth becomes creative power that will work for you.'"[16]

Yet that raises a difficult question: If the "Universe," the Supreme Intelligence, or God truly wants people to be wealthy, then why are so many impoverished? Why are there so few wealthy people if all that is necessary is for one to think or speak positively about and focus upon wealth? If, as Wattles and *The Secret* teach, the wealthy are rich because they have manipulated the universe through their thinking (or, as Word-Faith proponents would say, because of their words), then doesn't it also stand to reason that the poor must be blamed for their own poverty?

On this point *Salon* reporter Peter Birkenhead has rightly observed:

...with survivors of Auschwitz still alive, Oprah writes this about "The Secret" on her Web site, "the energy you put into the world—both good and bad—is exactly what comes back to you. This means you create the circumstances of your life with the choices you make every day...." Oprah, in the age of AIDS, is advertising a book that says, "You cannot 'catch' anything unless you think you can, and thinking you can is inviting it to you with your thought...." from a studio within walking distance of Chicago's notorious Cabrini Green Projects, [she] pitches a book that says, "The only reason any person does not have enough money is because they are blocking money from coming to them with their thoughts."[17]

> *It is the law of attraction. It says that the energy, that the thoughts and the feelings that you put out into the world, both good and bad, are exactly what is always coming back to you, so you have the life that you have created.*[18]
>
> OPRAH WINFREY

> *You create your life. Whatever you sow, you reap! Your thoughts are seeds, and the harvest you reap will depend on the seeds you plant.*
>
> *If you are complaining, the law of attraction will powerfully bring into your life more situations for you to complain about....*
>
> *The law is simply reflecting and giving back to you exactly what you are focusing on with your thoughts.*[19]
>
> RHONDA BYRNE

> *The words you speak are seeds that produce after their kind. Just as sure as they are planted, you can be equally sure a harvest will follow.... Now let's bring this in to*

focus. IT (poverty) should obey you. You said, "We don't ever have enough money. We will never be able to make the payments"; and IT (poverty) followed you home. You sneezed and said, "I am taking a cold" AND IT (the cold) was obedient to your words and the virus fastened itself to your body.[20]

CHARLES CAPPS, CHRISTIAN PROSPERITY TEACHER

GETTING WHATEVER YOU WANT

The knowledge *The Secret* claims to impart is much more than just how to obtain wealth. In fact, there appears nothing it cannot provide when one considers this testimonial from the book's foreword:

> As the film swept the world, stories of miracles began to flood in: people wrote about healing from chronic pain, depression, and disease; walking for the first time after an accident; even recovering from a deathbed. We have received thousands of accounts of The Secret getting used to bring about large sums of money and unexpected checks in the mail. People have used The Secret to manifest their perfect homes, life partners, cars, jobs, and promotions, with many accounts of businesses being transformed within days of applying The Secret. There have been heart-warming stories of stressed relationships involving children being restored to harmony.[21]

Wattles would agree that all these things are made possible by the Law of Attraction; however, he doesn't try to hide the fact that, first and foremost, it must be about acquiring wealth. Consider the following quotes from the book that Byrne claims changed her life:

> If you lack for physical health, you will find that the attainment of it is conditional on your getting rich. Only those who are emancipated from financial worry, and who have

the means to live a care-free existence and follow hygienic practices, can have and retain health.[22]

Moral and spiritual greatness is possible only to those who are above the competitive battle for existence; and only those who are becoming rich on the plane of creative thought are free from the degrading influences of competition.[23]

You can aim at nothing so great or noble, I repeat, as to become rich; and you must fix your attention upon your mental picture of riches, to the exclusion of all that may tend to dim or obscure the vision.[24]

OTHER SOURCES THAT INFLUENCED BYRNE

While *The Science of Getting Rich* was Byrne's introduction to the secret, Byrne relied upon many other related books in developing *The Secret*. As she shared with Oprah, "I read hundreds of books. I listened to hundreds of hours of audio. I was on the Internet. In two-and a-half weeks, I had traced The Secret back through history. Since I discovered The Secret, every single moment of my entire life has changed, and I am living my life for the first time."[25]

Who wrote these other books? Based on Byrne's acknowledgments and the quotes and attributions in *The Secret,* some of them were the writings of contemporaries of Wattles, or like-minded New Thought practitioners.

- *Who were these authors?*
- *Did they teach the secret?*
- *How much influence did they have on Byrne?*

To answer these questions, we must consider the secret architects.

THE SECRET ARCHITECTS

Visualization is a process that has been taught by all the great teachers and avatars throughout the centuries, as well as by all the great teachers living today. In Charles Haanel's book The Master Key System, *written in 1912, he gives twenty-four weekly exercises to master visualization. (More important, his complete* Master Key System *will also help you become the master of your thoughts.)*[1]

RHONDA BYRNE, AUTHOR OF *THE SECRET*

We have come to know that thinking is a spiritual process, that vision and imagination preceded action and event, that the day of the dreamer has come. The following lines by Mr. Herbert Kaufman are interesting in this connection. "They are the architects of greatness, their vision lies within their souls, they peer beyond the veils and mists of doubt and pierce the walls of unborn Time."[2]

CHARLES HAANEL, AUTHOR OF *THE MASTER KEY SYSTEM*

In the acknowledgments section of *The Secret,* Rhonda Byrne expresses gratitude to "every person who has come into my life and inspired, touched, and illuminated me through their presence."[3] Those whom she specifically mentions include "the great avatars and master teachers from the past, whose writings lit a burning fire of desire within me." She follows this with, "I have walked in the shadows of their greatness, and I honor every one of them. Special thanks to Robert Collier and Robert Collier Publications, Wallace Wattles, Charles Haanel, Joseph Campbell and the Joseph Campbell Foundation, Prentice Mulford, Genevieve Behrend, and Charles Fillmore."[4]

All the above-named individuals except Joseph Campbell (who was born in 1904) were born in the nineteenth century. Interestingly, Byrne identifies more than 80 people, by name, for whom she is grateful. Was it an ancient secret that linked these teachers born in the nineteenth century? Or were all these people associated, to some degree, as students, teachers, or writers of a view being popularized in the mid to late 1800s known as New Thought?[5] Who were these individuals, and what role did they and their beliefs in New Thought play in the production of *The Secret*? Did they really share Byrne's secret, or were they simply the architects whose plans she found and built upon?

Keep in mind that while Byrne did draw from Wallace Wattles's book *The Science of Getting Rich,* Wattles's book only started her journey. His was not the main course, but simply the New Thought "appetizer." Let's take a closer look at some of the individuals who influenced Byrne's thinking.

> *My greatest insights into The Secret on the subject of the world came from the teachings of Robert Collier, Prentice Mulford, Charles Haanel, and Michael Bernard Beckwith.*[6]
>
> RHONDA BYRNE

NEW THOUGHT TEACHERS AND THEIR INFLUENCE

PRENTICE MULFORD (1834–1891)

While Byrne may have found much insight from Prentice Mulford (1834–1891) he remains a rather obscure figure. As one New Thought Web site notes, "Although Prentice Mulford was one of the earliest pioneers of the New Thought teaching, he is still comparatively little known or read, chiefly on account of the high price of the six volumes known as 'The White Cross Library.' "[7] There are relatively few quotes attributed to Mulford in Byrne's book, and all but one of these is from *The God in You*.[8]

One quote is this:

> When you say to yourself, "I am going to have a pleasant visit or a pleasant journey," you are literally sending elements and forces ahead of your body that will arrange things to make your visit or journey pleasant.... Our thoughts, or in other words, our state of mind, is ever at work "fixing up" things good or bad in advance.[9]

Byrne expresses fascination over the fact that "Prentice Mulford wrote those words in the 1870s. What a pioneer! You can see clearly how important it is to *think in advance* every event in every day."[10]

While Mulford was a pioneer in the area of New Thought, others who followed would go much farther down the trail, including Robert Collier.

ROBERT COLLIER (1885–1950)

After being cured of a seemingly undiagnosable illness through Christian Science, Robert Collier concluded,

> If [the Mind] had dominion over his physical self, why could it not cure business problems too? Why could it not correct any financial lack? Why could it not bring him anything of good he might wish? [In answering this] he studied

hundreds of books and courses on everything relating to metaphysics, the occult, and success in life. Whole religions seemed to be built on it. He delved into the deepest mysteries of the Masters. It was a long time before he began to find parts that were really workable in everyday life; a long time before he realized tangible results from his efforts; but when results began, they came quickly.[11]

Of Collier's works Byrne wrote, "All of his books...were founded on Collier's own extensive research into metaphysics and on his personal belief that success, happiness, and abundance are easily and rightfully attainable by everyone."[12] Attainable as these are said to be, obviously, not everyone has them. As we have already seen, it is all a matter of one's choices. Or, as Byrne also quotes Collier, "If you have any lack, if you are prey to poverty or disease, it is because you do not believe or do not understand the power that is yours. It is not a question of the Universal giving to you. It offers everything to everyone—there is no partiality."[13]

Collier wrote extensively on his views, and his writings are readily accessible through the family-run Robert Collier Foundation. That his family continues to be involved in maintaining and distributing his work makes him somewhat unique among the secret architects named by Byrne. However, as with Mulford, Byrne cites relatively few quotes from Collier in her book, and all of them are from one source, *The Secret of the Ages*.

CHARLES HAANEL (1866–1949)

Based on the number of times Charles Haanel is quoted and because he is the first among these writers to use the term *Law of Attraction* (in sources Byrne mentions as having studied), he must be given special attention. Every quote by Haanel that is cited in Byrne's book comes from a single source: *The Master Key System*, which was written in 1912. This book is regarded as the most well-known of his writings, and in it one finds Haanel's development of what he refers to as the Law of Attraction.

Based upon this book's teachings, Byrne concludes, "Almost one hundred years ago, without the benefit of all the scientific discoveries of the last hundred years, Charles Haanel knew how the Universe operated."[14] She then quotes from page 86 of *The Master Key System:*

> The Universal Mind is not only intelligence, but it is substance, and this substance is the attractive force which brings electrons together by the law of attraction so they form atoms; the atoms in turn are brought together by the same law and form molecules; molecules take objective forms and so we find that the law is the creative force behind every manifestation, not only of atoms, but of worlds, of the Universe, of everything of which the imagination can form any conception.[15]

Were these dynamics that would later be proved by "scientific discoveries" just the wishful thinking of the new secret-sharers? Whether scientific or not, Byrne is correct in associating Haanel and Wattles. One cannot help but be reminded of Wattles when reading passages like this from Haanel:

> This, then, is the way we are consistently creating and recreating ourselves; we are today the result of our past thinking, and we shall be what we are thinking today, the Law of Attraction is bringing to us, not the things we should like, or the things we wish for, or the things some one else has, but it brings us "our own," the things which we have created by our thought processes, whether consciously or unconsciously.[16]

If this is true, then, as is the case with Wattles's teaching, the logical conclusion is that those who are sick, suffering, and impoverished are in that condition because of their own mental failures. Haanel explains it this way:

> If you require Wealth a realization of the fact that the "I" in you is one with the Universal mind which is all substance,

and is Omnipotent, will assist you in bringing into opera-
tion the law of attraction which will bring you into vibration
with those forces which make for success and bring about
conditions of power and affluence in direct proportion with
the character and purpose of your affirmation.[17]

"Vibration" here is critical. As Haanel elaborates, "The Law of Attraction
rests on vibration, which in turn rests upon the law of love."[18] In fact, he
would write that nothing is more powerful. "The vibrations of Mental
forces are the finest and consequently the most powerful in existence."[19]

Byrne surely picked up on this for *The Secret,* as is evident in these words:

Here is the "wow" factor. When you think about what
you want, and you emit that frequency, you cause the
energy of what you want to vibrate at that frequency and
you bring it to You! As you focus on what you want, you
are changing the vibration of the atoms of that thing, and
you are causing it to vibrate *to* You. The reason you are
the most powerful transmission tower in the Universe
is because you have been given the power to focus your
energy through your thoughts and alter the vibrations of
what you are focused on, which then magnetically draws
it to you.[20]

The use of the terms *atoms, molecules, electrons, vibrations, frequency,* and
transmission towers, among other similar words, certainly seems to lend
a scientific ring to what Haanel is teaching. But is he truly referring to
science when he uses terms like *Universal Mind* and *law of attraction,* or
is he simply putting forth ideas that come from New Thought proponents
such as Wattles?

WILLIAM WALLACE ATKINSON (1862–1932)
THE UNNAMED ARCHITECT?

Though Byrne doesn't mention it, her exhaustive reading on this subject is likely to have included the book *Thought Vibration: The Law of Attraction in the Thought World*, which was written by William W. Atkinson and published in 1906. In this book Atkinson contends,

> We speak learnedly of the Law of Gravitation, but ignore that equally wonderful manifestation, THE LAW OF ATTRACTION IN THE THOUGHT WORLD. We are familiar with that wonderful manifestation of Law which draws and holds together the atoms of which matter is composed—we recognize the power of the law that attracts bodies to the earth, that holds the circling worlds in their places, but we close our eyes to *the mighty law that draws to us the things we desire or fear, that makes or mars our lives.*[21]

Atkinson explains,

> We are sending out thoughts of greater or less intensity all the time, and we are reaping the results of such thoughts. Not only do our thought waves influence ourselves and others, but they have a drawing power—they attract to us the thoughts of others, things, circumstances, people, "luck," in accord with the character of the thought uppermost in our minds.[22]

Not unexpectedly, this is all related to "vibrations."

Remember, to illustrate the "wow factor" of the Law of Attraction, Byrne used the analogy of a transmission tower. And though Atkinson would not have understood a transmission tower in the same way as modern readers, it is interesting to note the similarity present in his own illustration from 1906:

> You will be able to carry this idea more clearly if you will think of the Marconi wireless instruments, which receive the vibrations only from the sending instrument which has been attuned to the same key, while other telegrams are passing through the air in near vicinity without affecting

the instrument. The same law applies to the operations of thought. We receive only that which corresponds to our mental attunement.[23]

One might think with all this discussion of science that this must have been a popular topic of discussion and investigation among the scientists of that day. But was that the case, or was it those outside the scientific community who were writing about and promoting these theories? Consider the following excerpt from another book by Atkinson, *Practical Mental Influence,* published in 1908:

> On the one hand we see and hear of the mighty power for good Mental Influence is exerting among the people today, raising up the sick, strengthening the weak, putting courage into the despondent and making successes of failures. But on the other hand the hateful selfishness and greed of unprincipled persons in taking advantage of this mighty force of nature and prostituting it to their own hateful ends, without heeding the dictates of conscience or the teaching of religion or morality. These people are sowing a baleful wind that will result in their reaping a frightful whirlwind on the mental plane. They are bringing down upon themselves pain and misery in the future.[24]

Who were some of those Atkinson refers to as using the power of mental influence? Atkinson provides interesting insight:

> What is known as a "Mental Image" in occultism, is the mental creation, in the imagination of a "picture" of the things, events or conditions that one desires to be manifested or materialized in actual effect. A moment's thought will show you that unless you know "just what" you desire, you can take no steps toward attaining it on any plane of manifestation....[25]

> It would surprise many people if they knew that some of the multi-millionaires of the country, and some of its

greatest politicians and leaders, were secret students of Occultism, and who were using their forces upon the masses of the people....[26]

The occult masters have ever impressed upon their pupils the importance and necessity of acquiring the power of Mental Concentration and all trained and developed occultists have practiced and persevered toward this end, the result being that some of them attained almost miraculous mental powers and influence. All occult phenomena are caused in this way, and all occult power depends upon it....[27]

And besides these, there are a number of people who have studied at the feet of some of the great metaphysical, semi-religious cults of the day, who have received instruction in Mental Influence disguised under the name of some creed or religious teachings, who have departed from the moral principles inculcated by their teachers, and who are using their knowledge in the shape of "treatments" of other persons for the purpose of influencing them to accede to their wishes.... The air is full of this Black Magic today, and it is surely time that the general masses were instructed on this subject.[28]

Atkinson candidly acknowledges the association of mental influence with metaphysics and occultism—and don't forget he writes as one who is actively involved in promoting the beliefs and practices of both New Thought and Hinduism.[29] Obviously the concepts he refers to—and that Byrne would later call the secret—were actually topics of discussion not among scientists of Wattles's day, but among those involved in occultism, New Thought, metaphysics, and the like.

Even Wattles was aware of this. He warned

...postpone your investigations into the occult. Do not dabble in theosophy, Spiritualism, or kindred studies. It is very likely that the dead still live, and are near; but if they are, let them alone; mind your own business...solve your own problem; get rich. If you begin to mix with the occult, you will start mental cross-currents which will surely bring your hopes to shipwreck.[30]

The monistic theory of the universe—the theory that One is All, and that All is One; that one Substance manifests itself as the seeming many elements of the material world—is of Hindu origin, and has been gradually winning its way into the thought of the western world for two hundred years. It is the foundation of all the Oriental philosophies, and of those of Descartes, Spinoza, Leibnitz, Schopenhauer, Hegel, and Emerson.[31]

You must lay aside all other concepts of the universe than this monistic one; and you must dwell upon this until it is fixed in your mind, and has become your habitual thought. Read these creed statements over and over again; fix every word upon your memory, and meditate upon them until you firmly believe what they say. If a doubt comes to you, cast it aside as a sin. Do not listen to arguments against this idea; do not go to churches or lectures where a contrary concept of things is taught or preached. Do not read magazines or books which teach a different idea; if you get mixed up in your faith, all your efforts will be in vain.[32]

WALLACE WATTLES

THE LACK OF SCIENTIFIC EVIDENCE

Though the architects of the secret try to lay claim for a basis in science, the evidence just isn't there. As we have seen, the more one investigates these claims, the more any credible scientific basis disappears. Even Wattles acknowledged this when he wrote, "Do not ask why these things are true, nor speculate as to how they can be true; simply take them on trust. The science of getting rich begins with the absolute acceptance of *this* faith" (emphasis added).[33]

As the layers are pulled back, the Law of Attraction seems more and more to be rooted not in science, but in the supernatural, or the spiritual. Is that also true of *The Secret* and its modern-day teachers?

- *Who are the modern secret-sharers?*

- *Where did they get their message?*

- *Is their message the same one that was taught by architects of the modern-day secret?*

To find out, we must first consider the secret link.

THE SECRET LINK

My greatest insights into The Secret on the subject of the world came from the teachings of Robert Collier, Prentice Mulford, Charles Haanel, and Michael Bernard Beckwith.[1]

RHONDA BYRNE, AUTHOR OF *THE SECRET*

You attract to you the predominant thoughts that you're holding in your awareness, whether those thoughts are conscious or unconscious. That's the rub.[2]

We're not speaking about religiosity. We're talking about our real identity which is a spiritual being.[3]

And we're here to unfold to become more aware of that and allow that energy to be released. The love, the peace, the joy, the wisdom, the harmony, these are all qualities of the spirit that is seeking to express through us, and so as we become more awake, more aware of that, our life is filled with that kind of vibration, that kind of feeling tone. So to grow spiritually is to actually become more aware of who you really are.[4]

MICHAEL BERNARD BECKWITH, FOUNDER OF AGAPE
INTERNATIONAL SPIRITUAL CENTER

When Rhonda Byrne set out to film *The Secret* DVD, she said she left Australia for the United States without a single teacher having been secured to appear in the film. According to Byrne, within seven weeks, her production team had filmed over 55 teachers,[5] 24 of whom are also featured in the book by the same title. Of the four teachers whom she has said provided her with the greatest insight into the secret, only one—Michael Bernard Beckwith—appears on *The Secret* DVD.

This is not to say that the other secret-sharers are of less importance than him. However, Beckwith must be given careful attention due to the special role he played in Byrne's understanding of the secret.

THE LINK TO MICHAEL BECKWITH

Beckwith says he was a drug dealer who was making thousands of dollars a week[6] prior to embarking on "an inward journey into the teachings of East and West" during the 1970s.[7] In 1985 he was ordained as a minister of Religious Science.[8] The following year he founded the Agape International Spiritual Center, which is described on the Agape Web site as "a trans-denominational movement and community of 9,000 local members and 1,000,000 friends worldwide."[9]

> *I was having a spiritual awakening. I actually died in a dream, and when I woke up, I could see things very differently. I could see that we were surrounded by this presence that I called love beauty that was everywhere.... The presence loved me at my core totally and completely, and it was the most beautiful beyond description. And this presence is everywhere. Most people say that God, or the presence is in everything, but in truth, everything is in the presence, and that totally changed my life.*[10]
>
> MICHAEL BERNARD BECKWITH

Beckwith also has one other notable distinction among those whom Byrne credits with providing the greatest insight into the secret—only

Beckwith is not among the late nineteenth and early twentieth-century New Thought teachers who influenced her. Yet his teachings are rooted in New Thought tradition.

The Agape Web site states that the center "teaches universal truth principles found in the New Thought-Ancient Wisdom tradition of spirituality."[11] In the frequently asked questions section of the Agape Web site, the question as to whether they are Christian is answered in this way, and is very telling as to Beckwith's "spiritual" heritage:

> No, and yes.... No, if by Christian you mean the acceptance of Jesus as the only savior and Christianity as the only path to God and eternal salvation. Yes, in the sense that New Thought-Ancient Wisdom history includes the Gnostic teachings of the earliest Christian mystical sects, as well as the founders of the uniquely American New Thought Movement including Emmanuel Swedenborg, Ernest Holmes, Howard Thurman, and transcendentalists such as Ralph Waldo Emerson and others.[12]

The list contains some of the same names associated with the architects of the secret. As is the case with Byrne, could Beckwith have a connection to them? The answer may be found in the person of Ernest Holmes, the founder of the Religious Science movement.

THE LINK TO ERNEST HOLMES (1887–1960)

Like Wattles, Haanel, Mulford, and Collier, Holmes had his feet firmly planted in the teachings of New Thought. Like so many of the New Thought leaders, he was acquainted with Christian Science and the writings of its founder, Mary Baker Eddy. Later, after reading the writings of Ralph Waldo Emerson, his interest in metaphysics was piqued, and he soon was exploring the writings of Christian D. Larson, Ralph Waldo Trine, Horatio Dresser, and Phineas Quimby. Holmes was particularly impressed with the New Thought writings of Larson and eventually abandoned the Christian Science textbook for Larson's works.[13]

Holmes visited his brother in California in 1912 and eventually moved to Los Angeles. There, he continued his religious studies and lectured on his views. He published his first book, *Creative Mind*, in 1919. A prolific writer, his best-known work, and the basis for the Religious Science movement, *The Science of Mind*, was published in 1926. The following year he incorporated the Institute of Religious Science and School of Philosophy and began a monthly publication to promote the teachings of the organization.[14] That magazine, *Science of Mind*,[15] is still published today.

Through his organization and writings, Holmes continues to exert an influence long after his death. As he once said, "We have launched a Movement which, in the next 100 years, will be the great new religious impulsion of modern times, far exceeding, in its capacity to envelop the world, anything that has happened since Mohammedanism started."[16]

That influence is especially being seen today through the attention given secret-tellers such as Beckwith. In an interview with Beckwith in the December 1996 issue of *Science of Mind* magazine, the interviewer notes, "Dr. Ernest Holmes writes in *The Science of Mind* that 'as we bring ourselves to a greater vision, we induce a greater concept and thereby demonstrate more in our experience. In this way there is a continuous growth and unfoldment taking place.' Beckwith teaches Holmes's ideas, offering practical guidance and specific techniques related to these ideas."[17]

> *This is a feeling Universe. If you just intellectually believe something, but you have no corresponding feeling underneath that, you don't necessarily have enough power to manifest what you want in your life. You have to feel it.*[18]

> *Scripturally we could say that we are the image and the likeness of God. We could say we are another way that the Universe is becoming conscious of itself. We could say that we are the infinite field of unfolding possibility. All of that would be true.*[19]

> *Are there any limits to this? Absolutely not. We are unlim-*
> *ited beings. We have no ceiling. The capabilities and the*
> *talents and the gifts and the power that is within every*
> *single individual that is on the planet, is unlimited.*[20]
>
> MICHAEL BERNARD BECKWITH

Beckwith wasn't an unknown prior to all the hype surrounding *The Secret*. However, his appearance in and promotion of *The Secret* has helped to increase his presence and following. Appearances on programs such as *Larry King Live* and *The Oprah Winfrey Show* have also afforded him a much larger forum. For example, nothing indicates his secret-marketability more than his invitation to return for a second appearance on *The Oprah Winfrey Show,* during which he told her that after his first appearance on the show, his personal Web site got over a million hits.[21]

Possibly even more impressive is the fact that Oprah told Beckwith that he phrased gratitude in a way that she had never heard it, going so far as to say, "When I heard that for the first time, my eyes watered, 'cause I thought just the way you phrased that it's, it connected.... I think that is an amazing view."[22] This is from someone who professes to have been a student and teacher of these principles for over 20 years.

Byrne chose her secret link well. Beckwith is not only a connection back to the nineteenth-century New Thought teachers, but has also proven that he can successfully connect to present-day secret-searchers as well. However, he does not provide any link to modern science.

But what about the other secret-tellers? Do they provide us with links to twenty-first-century science? Or do they, too, take us back to nineteenth-century spirituality?

- *Is there a common connection between the* Secret *teachers?*

- *Are they all connected to the New Thought teachers of previous centuries?*

- *Why do they promote* The Secret?

SIX DEGREES OF HAANEL

Almost one hundred years ago, without the benefit of all the scientific discoveries of the last hundred years, Charles Haanel knew how the Universe operated.[1]

RHONDA BYRNE, AUTHOR OF *THE SECRET*

All agree that there is but one Principle or Consciousness pervading the entire Universe, occupying all space, and being essentially the same in kind at every point of its presence. It is all powerful, all wisdom and always present. All thoughts and things are within Itself. It is all in all.... As this Consciousness is omnipresent, it must be present within every individual; each individual must be a manifestation of that Omnipotent, Omniscient and Omnipresent Consciousness.... As there is only one Consciousness in the Universe that is able to think it necessarily follows that your consciousness is identical with the Universal Consciousness, or, in other words, all mind is one mind. There is no dodging this conclusion.[2]

CHARLES HAANEL, NEW THOUGHT AUTHOR

During the 1990s, a group of college students invented a popular trivia game known as Six Degrees of Kevin Bacon. Though there have been subsequent variations, the game's original concept was to challenge players to take an actor from any period and see how quickly he or she can be connected to film star Kevin Bacon through their films. The goal is to do so in less than six films or actors—"six degrees"—and the number of actors it takes is known as a Bacon number. For example, Elvis Presley was in *Change of Habit* with Edward Asner, and Asner was in *JFK* with Kevin Bacon. Therefore, Elvis Presley has a Bacon number of 2.[3]

SIX DEGREES OF CHARLES HAANEL

Using this game as a model, what would happen if Charles Haanel were substituted for Kevin Bacon and the goal were to connect the modern secret teachers to Charles Haanel? If we were to play such a game, would it lead us back to the teachers of the late nineteenth and early twentieth centuries who framed the concepts behind what is now being called the secret? And, if it did, what would those modern teachers' Haanel number be?

Let's take some of the more popular and well-known secret teachers and see what happens. Let's play the Six Degrees of Charles Haanel.

BOB PROCTOR

Of Byrne's secret-tellers, Bob Proctor seems to have prominence in the DVD and is quoted more in the book than any of the others. Proctor's biography in *The Secret* states, "Bob Proctor's wisdom came to him through a lineage of great teachers. It began with Andrew Carnegie who passed it to Napoleon Hill, and then Hill passed it to Earl Nightingale. Earl Nightingale then passed the torch of wisdom to Bob Proctor."[4]

Napoleon Hill (1883–1970) wrote a number of motivational and personal success publications and books. Hill also claimed to be involved with spirit-beings,[5] which would certainly be a practice in common with some of the modern *Secret* teachers, such as the Hickses, but does he connect back to Haanel? In 1919 (after having achieved tremendous success working alongside Andrew Carnegie), Hill wrote a letter to Charles Haanel, stating in part,

> I believe in giving credit where it is due, therefore I believe I ought to inform you that my present success and the success which has followed my work as President of the Napoleon Hill Institute is due largely to the principles laid down in The Master-Key System. You are doing a good work by helping people to realize that nothing is impossible of accomplishment which a man can create in his imagination.[6]

From Proctor to Nightingale to Hill to Haanel gives Bob Proctor a Haanel number of 3.

> *You will attract everything that you require. If it's money you need you will attract it. If it's people you need you'll attract it. If it's a certain book you need you'll attract it.*[7]
>
> *Why do you think that 1 percent of the population earns around 96 percent of all the money that's being earned? Do you think that's an accident? It's designed that way. They understand something. They understand The Secret, and now you are being introduced to The Secret.*[8]
>
> BOB PROCTOR

JACK CANFIELD

Probably the best known of the secret teachers is Jack Canfield, who, with Victor Mark Hanson, has produced the Chicken Soup series of books. According to Canfield, his mentor W. Clement Stone "helped me realize that my then-current job—teaching high school history in an all-black school on the south side of Chicago—limited me to impacting just 30 lives a year."[8]

Stone was the founder of Combined Insurance Company of America and associated the company with Napoleon Hill from 1952 to 1962. There, Hill taught Stone's "Philosophy of Personal Achievement" and lectured on the "Science of Success."[10] Hill, of course, was associated with Haanel. So from Canfield to Stone to Hill to Haanel results in a Haanel number of 3 for Jack Canfield.

> *Since I learned The Secret and started applying it to my life, my life has truly become magical. I think the kind of life that everybody dreams of is one I live on a day-to-day basis. I live in a four-and-a-half-million-dollar mansion. I have a wife to die for. I get to vacation in all the fabulous spots of the world. I've climbed mountains. I've explored. I've been on safaris. And all of this happened, and continues to happen, because of knowing how to apply The Secret.[11]*
>
> JACK CANFIELD

NEALE DONALD WALSCH

Another superstar among the secret-tellers is Neale Donald Walsch. Of the group, he is second only to Canfield in the number of books sold, with each release of his *Conversations with God* series achieving best-seller status. Byrne's book refers to him as "a modern-day spiritual messenger…[who]…travels the world carrying the message of a New Spirituality."[12] What is that message, and from whom did he learn it?

In a 2000 interview with *Nexus* magazine, Walsch was asked about the teachers who influenced him. He replied, "If I were to name a few that had enormous impact on me, I would say Werner Erhard, Terry Cole Whitaker, Elizabeth Kübler-Ross, the Catholic Archbishop of Chicago, now deceased, my mother, Barbara Marks Hubbard, Carl Rogers and Buckminster Fuller."[13] This is quite a varied list, but one with some common "spiritual" threads to others in *The Secret*. Elizabeth Kübler-Ross was at one time extensively involved in channeling, and Terry Cole Whitaker is a graduate of the Ernest Holmes School of Religion and an ordained minister of the United Church of Religious Science. Those get us close to Haanel, but the founder of est, Werner Erhard, gets us all the way.

"William Warren Bartley III (*Werner Erhard: the Transformation of a Man*) tells us that Erhard was 'profoundly dissatisfied with the competitive and meaningless status quo' and was deeply affected by Napoleon Hill's *Think and Grow Rich*."[14] Napoleon Hill, of course, was deeply affected by Charles Haanel; therefore, Walsch to Erhard to Hill to Haanel gives us a Haanel number of 3 for Neale Donald Walsch.

> *So your purpose is what you say it is. Your mission is the mission you give yourself. Your life will be what you create it as, and no one will stand in judgment of it, now or ever.*[15]
>
> NEALE DONALD WALSCH

JAMES ARTHUR RAY

While Ray does not yet have the renown and stature of Canfield or Walsch, he is certainly on the rise. He appeared with several other secret teachers, including Byrne, on *The Oprah Winfrey Show* and it was apparent in the show that much of the attention was being given to him and Beckwith. When Oprah decided to do a follow-up show the next week, the only secret teachers on the program were Ray and Beckwith.

Ray's biographical sketch in *The Secret* begins, "A student of the principles of true wealth and prosperity his entire life, James developed The Science of Success and Harmonic Wealth, which teaches people how to receive unlimited results in all areas: financially, relationally, intellectually, physically, and spiritually."[16] With this emphasis on wealth, surely there will be an association to Haanel.

In his book *The Science of Success,* Ray stresses the importance of having mentors. He describes these as "people who have already achieved a level of success to which you aspire, and to whom you can go for guidance and insight."[17] Concerning his own involvement with mentors he writes, "All highly successful individuals have had powerful teachers. I've had mentors since I was very young—and they have been some of the most powerful and significant forces in my life."[18] Who were these mentors, these powerful teachers?

The reader is not told, except for one reference that says, "My dear friend and mentor Bob Proctor once told me, 'Results tell an interesting story... they tell the true story.'"[19] Of course, Proctor, as we know, was mentored by Nightingale, who was mentored by Hill, who credited Haanel's work with playing an important role in his own success. Ray to Proctor to Nightingale to Hill to Haanel gives a Haanel number of 4 for James Arthur Ray.

> *If you think about Aladdin and his lamp, Aladdin picks up the lamp, dusts it off, and out pops the Genie. The Genie always says one thing...trace the story back to its origins there's absolutely no limit whatsoever to the wishes. Think about that one.*
>
> *Now, let's take this metaphor and apply it to your life. Remember Aladdin is the one who always asks for what he wants. Then you've got the Universe at large, which is the Genie. Traditions have called it so many things—your holy guardian angel, your higher self. We can put any label on it, and you choose the one that works best for you, but every tradition has told us there's something bigger than us.*
>
> *And the Genie always says one thing: "Your wish is my command!"*[20]
>
> JAMES ARTHUR RAY

IT'S NOT JUST A GAME

Six Degrees of Haanel might prove to be a fun game, but these secret-tellers aren't in this for the fun. They are serious about what they teach, and with plenty of reasons. In fact, one might say they have millions of reasons to be serious in their promotion of this so-called science.

As Jerry Adler noted,

> "The Secret" brings breathless pizzazz and a market-proven gimmick, an evocation of ancient wisdom and hidden conspiracies that calls to mind "The Da Vinci Code." Torchlights flicker on the 90-minute DVD and the soundtrack throbs portentously before it gets down to giving you the secret for getting your hands on that new BMW.... What it doesn't contain, though, is a secret. That should be self-evident to anyone who has ever been in an airport bookstore. The film and book are built around 24 "teachers," mostly motivational speakers and writers (dressed up by Byrne with titles like "philosopher" or "visionary") who have been selling the same message for years.[21]

Regardless of how they package it, no matter how well they promote it, and no matter how wealthy they may get from selling it, their message is just not about science. All the secrets they claim to have uncovered—the Law of Attraction, vibrations, magnetic polarity, the appeal to quantum physics, etc.—all of them bring us back to a hybrid conglomeration of religious perspectives that are rooted in Eastern traditions and being repackaged as what the secret-tellers call spirituality.

At least Wattles was more forthcoming when he wrote that "the theory that...one Substance manifests itself as the seeming many elements of the material world—is of Hindu origin, and has been gradually winning its way into the thought of the western world for two hundred years. It is the foundation of all the Oriental philosophies."[22] He then said, "You must lay aside all other concepts of the universe than this monistic one;

and you must dwell upon this until it is fixed in your mind, and has become your habitual thought."[23]

Wattles also made no pretense that it is really all about acquiring wealth. And while the secret-tellers keep insisting this will work for everyone, producing some thought-invoked utopia, the reality is most of the peoples of the world are still impoverished. And without the funds to buy DVD players and the book, they will remain unconscious of the fact that all they need to do is think away their suffering.

> *In the film, the Rev. Michael Bernard Beckwith compares it to the law of gravity: "If you fall off a building it doesn't matter if you're a good person or a bad person, you're going to hit the ground."*
>
> *Which is equally true if someone pushes you off a building— or, let's say, beats your brains in with a club during a bout of ethnic cleansing. The law of attraction implies that you brought that fate down on yourself as well. "The law of attraction is that each one of us is determining the frequency that we're on by what we're thinking and feeling," Byrne said in a telephone interview, in response to a question about the massacre in Rwanda. "If we are in fear, if we're feeling in our lives that we're victims and feeling powerless, then we are on a frequency of attracting those things to us...totally unconsciously, totally innocently, totally all of those words that are so important."[24]*
>
> JERRY ADLER, *NEWSWEEK*

MANY HAVE BEEN PERSUADED

Will people honestly suspend their critical thinking and just buy this lock, stock, and barrel? In this culture, you better believe it. As Peter Birkenhead has noted,

Somebody is buying enough copies of "The Secret" to make it No. 1 on the Amazon bestseller list. Those somebodies may be religious zealots or atheists, Republicans or Democrats, but they are all believers, to one degree or another.... And yes, sure, a lot of the believing they do is harmless fun—everybody's got some kind of rabbit's foot in his pocket—but we're not talking about rabbits' feet here, we're talking about whole, live rabbits pulled out of hats, and an audience that doesn't think it's being tricked. "Secret"-style belief is a perfect product. Like Coca-Cola, it goes down easy and makes the consumer thirsty for more.... This modern idea of faith isn't arrived at the old-fashioned way, by asking questions, but by getting answers. Instead of inquiry we have born-again epiphanies and cheesy self-help books—we have excuses for not engaging in inquiry at all. Let other people schlep down the road to Damascus; we'll have Amazon send Damascus to us.[25]

Whether the rest of the world is doing well or not, the secret-sellers seem to be doing okay. However, some of them, it seems, have been applying the Law of Attraction to the queen of the magnets.

- *Can the* Secret *teachers use their uncanny powers on Oprah and get her involved in* The Secret?
- *Why might* The Secret *appeal to Oprah?*
- *What does Oprah offer the* Secret *teachers?*

Let's move onward now to Oprah's *Secret* adventure.

15

OPRAH'S SECRET ADVENTURE

The Secret is a book and it's a DVD that really is touching a nerve around the world. The timing, I believe, is just perfectly right.[1]

OPRAH WINFREY, TALK SHOW HOST

By continuing to hawk "The Secret," a mishmash of offensive self-help clichés, Oprah Winfrey is squandering her goodwill and influence, and preaching to the world that mammon is queen.[2]

PETER BIRKENHEAD, NEWS REPORTER, SALON.COM

Though already highly successful (with over a million DVDs and books sold in its first year of availability), without question *The Secret*'s continued success was guaranteed when producer Rhonda Byrne and several of the secret-tellers were invited to appear on the February 8, 2007 airing of *The Oprah Winfrey Show*. Though somewhat late to the party (Byrne had already promoted the DVD/book on *Larry King Live* and *The Ellen Degeneres Show*), Oprah was now ready to jump on the bandwagon. Why?

According to Oprah, "I have to tell you, in one day, six people told me about [*The Secret*]. I mean—and I hadn't heard about it when the first person told me. By the time the sixth person told me, I go, Okay. I'm gonna go home. I'm gonna watch it tonight."[3] Not only did she watch it, but later in the show she told Byrne that after viewing *The Secret* she went out and bought 30 copies—no doubt, to pass along to others.

> The Secret *is a book and it's a DVD that really is touching a nerve around the world. The timing, I believe, is just perfectly right. I feel it that so many people are hungry for guidance and meaning in their lives, and The Secret offers some of that. It is the law of attraction. It says that the energy, that the thoughts and the feelings that you put out into the world, both good and bad, are exactly what is always coming back to you, so you have the life that you have created. I've been talking about this for years on my show, I just never called it The Secret.*[4]
>
> OPRAH WINFREY

> *Oprah Winfrey is one of the richest women in the world, and one of the most influential. Her imprimatur has helped the authors of "The Secret" sell 2 million books (and 1 million DVDs), putting it ahead of the new Harry Potter book on the Amazon bestseller list. In the time Oprah spent advertising the lies in "The Secret," she could have been exposing them to an audience that otherwise might have believed them.*[5]
>
> PETER BIRKENHEAD

WHO ATTRACTED WHOM?

Was it Oprah's newly found fascination with *The Secret* that brought her in, or was it due to the principles of the secret being used on her? At least two of the guests on the program said it was the latter, and indicated that Oprah had to do the show because they had "attracted" her to it. Here is how they expressed it in a partial transcript from the show:

> LISA NICHOLS (TEACHER OF "THE SECRET"): And it's important to—for me, create visuals. I love visuals to remind me of who I am, of where I'm going, of what I want. I created a—a visualization board, and I just put on it the things that I really wanted.... Right in the center, I don't know if they can close-up on it, but I cut out the words Lisa tells all on The Oprah Winfrey Show, right there...
>
> JAMES RAY (TEACHER OF "THE SECRET"): I did the same thing six years ago as Lisa did, put it out into the universe that I was gonna be on the show...and guess what? You guys called me.
>
> LISA NICHOLS: Right.
>
> OPRAH WINFREY (HOST): We called you. It works.[6]

Whether she intended to communicate this or not, Oprah's response is very telling as to one of the problems with the Law of Attraction—people can be manipulated to take actions based on the power of another's thoughts. Obviously, if Oprah were to be asked why she did a program on *The Secret,* she would not respond it was due to James Ray thinking he would be on her show, or because Lisa Nichols put some words on a visualization board. However, that is exactly what Lisa Nichols and James Ray are saying occurred.

> *The law of attraction is really obedient. When you think of the things that you want, and you focus on them with all of your intention, then the law of attraction will give you*

> *exactly what you want, every time.... When you focus on*
> *something, no matter what it happens to be, you really are*
> *calling that into existence.*[7]
>
> *You can see the law of attraction everywhere. You draw*
> *everything to yourself. The people, the job, the circum-*
> *stances, the health, the wealth, the debt, the joy, the car*
> *that you drive, the community that you're in. And you've*
> *drawn them all to you, like a magnet. What you think*
> *about you bring about. Your whole life is a manifestation*
> *of the thoughts that go on in your head.*[8]
>
> LISA NICHOLS

In reality it was not the cosmic thoughts of these secret-tellers that brought Oprah to *The Secret*. Rather, like a moth drawn to light, Oprah has embraced *The Secret* because it expresses a philosophy of living and an ideology with which she is already most comfortable. As she shared with her audience,

> ...this is a happy, happy day for me, 'cause all my life, I wanted to be a teacher. And I've known "The Secret"—I didn't call it "The Secret" for years. And for years on this show, this is what I've been trying to do, is to get people to see it through different ways manifested through the lives of other people, being able to set examples for people. So this is really exciting that these teachers are here today to share it.[9]

And what was the message of *The Secret* that Oprah understood upon viewing the DVD—the message she has known and tried to get people to see "for years"? The following exchange with Rhonda Byrne is most revealing in answering this question:

> OPRAH WINFREY:...when I watched "The Secret," I realized I've always lived by the secret. I didn't know it was a secret.... Why do you call it "The Secret"?

RHONDA BYRNE: We really needed to contain the—contain the knowledge in, in a couple of words. And "The Secret" is the law of attraction.

OPRAH WINFREY: Okay. So what do you mean by that?

RHONDA BYRNE: The law of attraction I would describe as the most powerful law in the universe and it is the law by which we are creating our lives….we attract into our lives the things that we want, and that is based on what we're thinking and feeling…

OPRAH WINFREY: Yeah. So what you're saying is, is that we all—human beings here on Earth—create our own reality.

RHONDA BYRNE: We do.

OPRAH WINFREY: We create our own circumstances.

RHONDA BYRNE: Yes.

OPRAH WINFREY: We create our own circumstances by the choices that we make and the choices that we make are fueled by our thoughts. So our thoughts are the most powerful thing that we have here on Earth.

RHONDA BYRNE: They are. They are.

OPRAH WINFREY: And based upon what we think, and what we think determines who we are, we attract who we are into our lives.[10]

But where does such power come from—this power to create one's own reality by what one thinks? What is this "secret" Oprah has been teaching for years? Is it really the same as what Byrne refers to as the Law of Attraction?

So, an individual could actually begin to generate a certain feeling of gratitude, of love, of peace, and of harmony, and

> *the universe will begin to match that feeling tone, and what will flow into your life will match the feeling that you're holding. It's scientific. It's real.*[11]
>
> MICHAEL BERNARD BECKWITH

> *I am guided by a higher calling.... It's not so much a voice as it is a feeling. If it doesn't feel right to me, I don't do it.... It is easier to go with the river than to try to swim upstream. Anything negative that happens to me is because I've been fighting against the stream.*[12]
>
> OPRAH WINFREY

OPRAH'S "SECRET" POWER

During the early to mid 1990s Oprah's television program was a frequent stopover for a number of New Age or metaphysical teachers (many of whom were made famous by her endorsement), such as Marianne Williamson, Deepak Chopra, Gary Zukav, Iyanla Vanzant, Neale Donald Walsch, Eckhart Tolle, Shirley MacLaine, and Sophy Burnham. They would influence and lay the groundwork for the *Secret* teachers, with at least one, Walsch, later being recognized as a "Secret" teacher.

They brought with them a newly packaged self-help, feel-good kind of spirituality, some of which Oprah readily embraced. Their influence on her is evident by the fact Oprah lists some of their books on her Web site as being among her personal favorites.[13] Of one favorite book, *Discover the Power Within You* by deceased Unity Church leader Eric Butterworth, she states, "This book changed my perspective on life and religion. Eric Butterworth teaches that God isn't 'up there.' He exists inside each one of us, and it's up to us to seek the divine within."[14] Her favorite quote from the book is this: "...the greatest mistake is in believing that we are 'only human....' We are human in expression but divine in creation and limitless in potentiality."[15]

Oprah has acknowledged this period of her life as one of change, going so far as to say, "I would say 1994 was a time of profound change for me, emotionally, spiritually, and physically."[16] She was in the "flow."

> *The laws have been in existence long before anybody heard of* The Secret *or before that videotape. So, understanding, for me, understanding that the laws are true, that it really does work, that this is the way. What I've, what I've figured out is that you can struggle against the current of your life or you can figure out what the current is, the flow of your life, and turn around and be carried, literally carried, from one level to the next in your own life. You don't have to, when I see people struggling and so many difficulties all the time, I go turn around and find your flow. Find your flow.*[17]
>
> *Moving with the flow of life has given me supreme confidence because I know there's a Power greater than I, a natural rhythm to things that is a force beyond my own. I trust it and believe that no matter what, I will be okay.*[18]
>
> Oprah Winfrey

When Oprah reached her fiftieth birthday she concluded, "What I know for sure as I crest this major milestone: My life is bigger than I can ever know or imagine. It has its own force field. I can feel myself propelling it—guiding it, even. But most often I try to surrender to its own divine guidance."[19]

A guided meditation recommended by Oprah illustrates this point: "The universe is not interested in your struggles and your pain and your sorrow. It wants you to be joyful. We often struggle because we swim upstream. All that is God, my heart is open to you. My heart is open to find the flow, the flow, the flow, the flow that is my life."[20]

Is God Anywhere in This?

One might logically ask at this point, "So, is it our thoughts that create our reality—is it we who propel and guide our own life—or is it God, or some divine force?"

It seems mixed signals are being given on this point. In fact, during Oprah's second show with the *Secret* teachers, at least one audience member, who identified herself as a Christian, picked up on it and asked, "...it seems that *The Secret* teaches you to put your faith in yourself, and so I was wondering, is God anywhere in this?"[21]

Oprah acknowledged this was a great question and offered the following explanation:

...I've been on the spiritual path for a very long time...and that was the number one question I had, because I was raised a Christian. I still am a Christian. And the number one question I had was, how does all of this, you know, metaphysical thinking, this new way of taking responsibility for my life and co-creating my life with the creator, how does that mesh with everything that I've been taught? And what I realized is exactly what they're saying, is that it reinforces, because above all else, God gave us free will. He gave us the will to make choices in our life. And what The Secret is saying...what universal principles say is you have the free will, know that the choices that you make will always have a consequence, so choose wisely. That's how it's integrated for myself.[22]

This response doesn't really clarify the issue, for she postures that it is both we and the divine who establish the flow of life. Further muddying the waters is Oprah's representation that she holds to a Christian concept of God, thus implying that the view of God presented in *The Secret* is compatible with the view held by Christianity.

> *What I know is that God, nature, the Spirit, the universe, whatever title you wish to give him—or her—is always trying to help each one of us to be the best and do the best that we can.*[23]
>
> *I think you know what's so important to me is that God isn't a he or a she but is everything.*[24]

I believe in the FORCE—I call it God.[25]

OPRAH WINFREY

It is readily apparent that Oprah has correctly concluded that there is a spiritual basis being claimed for the Law of Attraction. Is she, and are the *Secret* teachers, also correct in associating that "force" as being the same as the God who is spoken of in the Bible and in other religions?

At least one who disagrees is Oprah's former pastor, Jeremiah Wright of Trinity United Church of Christ in Chicago. Wright has stated, "She has broken with the [traditional faith].... She now has this sort of 'God is everywhere, God is in me, I don't need to go to church, I don't need to be a part of a body of believers, I can meditate, I can do positive thinking' spirituality. It's a strange gospel. It has nothing to do with the church Jesus Christ founded."[26]

This leaves us with some significant unanswered questions:

- *Does metaphysical thinking "mesh" with Christianity, as described by Oprah?*

- *Is God in* The Secret, *and if so, who is God, according to* The Secret?

- *Did Jesus teach the secret?*

To find out, we must understand the "sacred" science of *The Secret*.

THE SACRED SECRET

The secret is within you…. [Y]ou will Be the Power, you will be the perfection, you will Be the wisdom, you will Be the intelligence….[1]

You are a spiritual being. You are energy, and energy cannot be created or destroyed—it just changes form. Therefore, the pure essence of you has always been and always will be.[2]

LISA NICHOLS

You are eternal life. You are God manifested in human form….[3]

RHONDA BYRNE

You will surely never die.
For the very moment you partake,
your eyes will become enlightened
then you shall be God.[4]

ANCIENT TEACHER, GENESIS 3:4-5, THE BIBLE

What is the secret?

Most readers of *The Secret* would probably say, "thoughts become things," or "Our minds are like powerful television transmitters," or perhaps "The Law of Attraction."

You may be surprised to learn that every one of those answers is wrong. While Rhonda Byrne does share these secrets in her book, they are not *the* secret.

So what is the *real* secret?

The casual reader will probably not catch it. Very few reviews of *The Secret* make mention of it. Most miss the main point.

The most powerful secret in the book is not the Law of Attraction. It has nothing to do with attracting necklaces or visualizing new sports cars. The main secret is not about quantum mechanical theories or curing cancer. The most significant secret is not even about creating world peace.

Those are just the minor secrets. Sure, those secrets attract your attention and stir your imagination. But if you remain focused on these secrets, you will miss the really big secret.

The lesser, minor secrets—the Law of Attraction, thoughts become things, thought transmission, and vibration—may be found in the first few pages of *The Secret*. Like a good author, Rhonda Byrne saves the big secret, the most important secret, for the closing sections of her book.

The *real* secret is not about *things,* it is about *you.* It is about your true nature.

It is the sacred secret.

One, None, Many, or All

What is the sacred secret? Before you can be entrusted with it, you must first understand the powerful nature of worldviews. Without learning the lesson of the worldviews, you will surely miss the sacred secret.

Worldviews are very powerful things that shape everything from our basic understanding of reality to our core values. Everything—all our assumptions, the way we function in society, our relationships—all these and more are governed by our worldview.

And there are four worldviews. They are the One, the None, the Many, and the All. Everyone holds to one of these worldviews. Which one do you hold to?

THE ONE

The first worldview is ONE. It is the worldview of most people in the Western world. It is called *monotheism*. This worldview holds to the idea of One (*mono*) God (*theos*). The core value for monotheists is the belief that there is one true God and every other God is a false god. Most people in Europe and the Americas are monotheists. This is the worldview of Judaism, Christianity, and Islam.

THE NONE

The second worldview is NONE. It is the worldview of *atheism*. Atheists believe in no (*a*) God (*theos*). They generally hold to a nonsupernatural, mechanistic view of reality. This worldview is also very powerful in Europe and the United States. It is the worldview of secular humanism.

THE MANY

The third worldview is MANY. It is the worldview known as *polytheism*. They believe in many (*poly*) Gods (*theos*). While this worldview has fallen out of popularity in Europe and the Americas, at one time it was the predominant worldview of the civilized world. Examples include the religion of the pharaohs in ancient Egypt as well as the mythology of the ancient Greeks with their gods and goddesses on Mount Olympus.

Rhonda Byrne's final secret—the sacred secret—is not in harmony with any of these first three worldviews. It emanates from the fourth view. For most Americans and Europeans, this worldview may seem puzzling or counter-intuitive. Perhaps this is why most readers miss the sacred secret.

THE ALL

The fourth worldview is ALL. It is the worldview of *pantheism.* Pantheists believe that all (*pan*) is God (*theos*). Their core values include the concept that everything is connected—all is one (monism)—and that one is God. Major religions from Asia and the East share the basic principles of pantheism. They include Hinduism, Taoism, and to some degree, Buddhism. As we have seen, this is also the fundamental philosophy underlying the Mind Science religions of the nineteenth century.

Pantheists generally believe that God is eternal yet impersonal. They usually refer to God as *It,* not *He.* They understand that everything we see—the whole cosmos—is interconnected and eternal. Everything—the snowflake, the blade of grass, the Peruvian rainforest, your next-door neighbor—is God.

If you understand this fourth worldview, the ALL, you are ready for the final secret—the sacred secret.

THE SACRED SECRET

Virtually every one of Byrne's secret principles (the positive affirmations, the uplifting illustrations, and the inspiring testimonials) is deeply rooted in pantheism. Because most who read *The Secret* are monotheists or atheists, initially these may seem like novel ideas and concepts. They are not. Perhaps this is why *The Secret* can seem to be both new and ancient at the same time.

The sacred secret is about you and your hidden identity. You have greatly underestimated yourself. Although there are hints earlier in the book, you don't learn the sacred secret until the final chapters.

The sacred secret is this: You are God.

If you are familiar with pantheism, then you would be able to see the clues scattered throughout *The Secret*.

Over two dozen times we learn that "You" are actually "the creator" and that "you create" things out of nothing. You don't just create your new sports car or exotic vacation. Because you are God, you create the universe.

> *So we are the creators, not only of our own destiny, but ultimately we are the creators of Universal destiny. We are the creators of the Universe. So there's no limit, really, to human potential.*[5]
>
> DR. JOHN HAGELIN, *THE SECRET*

This is why many atheists and skeptic organizations have been so critical of *The Secret*. It is not just the pseudoscience and irrational claims that bother them. They understand that *The Secret* is not just about gaining wealth or positive thinking. It is about religion. If there is no God, then how can we be God?

According to Byrne, however, there is a God, and You are It.

> *You are God in a physical body. You are Spirit in the flesh. You are Eternal Life expressing itself as You. You are a cosmic being. You are all power. You are all wisdom. You are all intelligence. You are perfection. You are magnificence. You are the creator, and you are creating the creation of You on this planet.*[6]
>
> RHONDA BYRNE

Many monotheists are even more deeply disturbed than the atheists are. Most appreciate the book's emphasis on gratitude, a positive mental attitude, and loving others. Monotheists certainly can identify with Rhonda Byrne's quest to find spiritual answers for life's biggest challenges.

Jews, Christians, and Muslims, however, are not very thrilled to discover that they are God. For them, this idea is not just wrong; it is offensive. For many, it is the worst kind of heresy. It is blasphemy.

Monotheists, and that includes many Americans and Europeans, believe that there is only one true God and that God is in heaven. Those who ascribe the attributes of deity to themselves (or claim that they are God) are violating the basic principles of monotheism.

Rabbi Benjamin Blech says that *The Secret* "offends not only my intelligence but also my faith."[7] Christians are also offended. It is not too surprising to learn that some nonreligious bookstores are now refusing to carry *The Secret* because its message clearly violates the Christian worldview.[8]

A SONG FOR YOU

The Secret even includes an affirmation that sounds like something from a Christian hymnbook. This praise and worship, however, is not directed toward the God of heaven. The object of this worship and adoration is You. This song is sung to You.

> *The earth turns on its orbit for You. The oceans ebb and flow for You. The birds sing for You. The sun rises and it sets for You. The stars come out for You. Every beautiful thing you see, every wondrous thing you experience, is all there, for You. Take a look around. None of it can exist, without You.*
>
> *No matter who you thought you were, now you know the Truth of Who You Really Are. You are the master of the Universe. You are the heir to the kingdom. You are the perfection of Life. And now you know The Secret.*[9]
>
> RHONDA BYRNE

Indeed, "now you know The Secret."

What began as a quest to attract more money, lose weight, and experience good health ends up as a religious conversion.

In order to receive the *true* secret—the sacred secret—you must take your rightful place on the throne as the Master of the universe. You must accept Yourself as Lord and Savior.

This is why Donald S. Whitney, a Christian seminary professor, says, "It is no exaggeration to say that [*The Secret*] implicitly (and sometimes explicitly) denies virtually every major doctrine in the Bible."[10]

Christians can find some common ground with Byrne. Like pantheists, Christians believe in the promise of eternal life. From their perspective, however, eternal life is not based on recognizing their own inherent nature as eternal energy or their identity as God. For them, God is a personal being—not a What, but a Who.

They understand God to be a distinct, personal, and eternal being who is all perfection. They see themselves neither as God nor as perfect. In fact, they understand themselves to be flawed and incomplete—incapable, under their own power, of saving themselves.

Most monotheists believe that they have failed, in some way, to keep God's laws. They believe in a coming judgment. *The Secret*, however, says that "no one will stand in judgment of [your life], now or ever."[11]

> *There's something magnificent about you…. The moment you begin to "think properly," this something that's within you, this power within you that's greater than the world, it will begin to emerge. It will take over your life. It will feed you. It will clothe you. It will guide you, protect you, direct you, sustain your very existence. If you let it.*[12]
>
> MICHAEL BERNARD BECKWITH

Monotheists can never truly accept *The Secret* without a radical religious conversion. For Christians particularly, salvation comes through recognizing their shortcomings and sin and placing their faith and trust in

Jesus Christ, who died on the cross to pay the penalty of their sin and who rose from the dead three days later. On their behalf, Christ conquered sin and the grave.

The Secret, however, implies that there is no sin, sickness, or death. Christians recognize Jesus as God in the flesh. *The Secret* says that you are God in the flesh.

THE SECRET IN THE GARDEN

Those who look to the Bible as the source of wisdom recognize an eerie parallel. This sacred secret sounds familiar—too familiar. It sounds very much like the secret promise shared with Eve in the Garden of Eden.[13]

Satan, appearing as a serpent in the Garden of Eden, tempted Eve to sin against God by eating of the forbidden fruit. This was the original sin.

If Eve would only disobey God and follow the serpent, he would grant her a promise—actually, three promises. The serpent promised Eve that:

- *She would not die. This is the promise of immortality and eternal life.*

- *Her eyes would be opened. This is the promise of enlightenment. She would learn a secret.*

- *She would be as God, knowing good and evil. This is the promise of deification. This is the sacred secret.*

From this biblical account, it seems Rhonda Byrne did get at least one thing right, The Secret is ancient. In fact, it is so old that it was the first secret ever hissed (shh!) into human ears—the promise that we are God. And this "secret" continues to live on—being whispered from one person to another throughout the ages. It is the secret promise of empowerment and spiritual fulfillment, the promise that you can control your own destiny, for you are God.

So now you know the truth behind *The Secret* and now you must decide:

- *Does it really deliver on its promise, or is it just a lure, an enticement from the truth?*

- *Is it really the true path, or is it simply an ancient temptation?*

- *Are you really God of the universe, or is there one more worthy than you who is the one true God?*

These are important questions to answer. Careful consideration should be given to them and to the claims of *The Secret* and its teachers, for in answering them you will write the final chapter.

> *I pray that the eyes of your heart may be enlightened, so that you will know what is the hope of His calling, what are the riches of the glory of His inheritance in the saints, and what is the surpassing greatness of His power toward us who believe. These are in accordance with the working of the strength of His might which He brought about in Christ, when He raised Him from the dead and seated Him at His right hand in the heavenly places, far above all rule and authority and power and dominion, and every name that is named, not only in this age but also in the one to come.*
>
> THE APOSTLE PAUL
> *EPHESIANS* 1:18-21, THE BIBLE

NOTES

CHAPTER 1—WHAT IS THE SECRET?

1. "The Power of Positive Thoughts," transcript from *Larry King Live,* November 2, 2006, http://transcripts.cnn.com/TRANSCRIPTS/0611/02/lkl.01.html.

2. Rahel Deahl, "Atria's 'Secret' Is Way Out of the Bag," *Publisher's Weekly,* March 1, 2007.

3. Rhonda Byrne, *The Secret* (New York: Atria Books, 2006), p. xi.

4. Press Release "The Secret Is Out...Publisher Orders 2,000,000 Additional Copies," http://www.simonsays.com/content/feature.cfm?sid=33&feature_id=5796.

5. Byrne, *The Secret,* pp. 45-46. The genie granting requests with the phrase "Your wish is my command" is a reoccurring theme throughout *The Secret.* Rhonda Byrne suggests that legends such as Aladdin's magic lamp and genie, contain in their essence, "the very truth of life." In *The Secret,* James Ray claims that the earliest (allegedly more accurate?) versions of the legend promise an unlimited number of desires and not just "three wishes." Ray explains the symbolism—the genie represents "the Universe at Large" granting all wishes according to the Law of Attraction. The actual origins of the term *genie* (spelled Jinn, Jinni, djinni, or djinn) dates back to pre-Islamic Arabia. According to James Robson, genies were considered to be a separate race of beings created out of "smokeless fire." Genies could potentially live very long lives and were believed to be able to reproduce themselves. Both good and evil genies were thought to exist. They were considered to be spirit beings who could assume the shape of animals or humans. In the Qur'an, Satan is called a jinn (Sura 18.50-51). In Western culture, they are often seen as tricksters who may grant wishes in such a way as to harm the wisher. (See: "Jinn," by James Robson in Richard Cavendish, ed., *Man, Myth, & Magic,* Vol. 11 [New York: Marshall Cavendish Corporation, 1970], p. 1516).

6. "One Week Later: The Huge Reaction to *The Secret,*" transcript from *The Oprah Winfrey Show,* February 16, 2007, http://www2.oprah.com/spiritself/slide/20070216/ss_20070216_284_103.jhtml.

7. "Customers' Reviews," Barnes & Noble, March 5, 2007, http://tinyurl.com/2wxz88.

8. Byrne, *The Secret*, p. 4.

CHAPTER 2—*THE SECRET SHARED*

1. As cited in Rhonda Byrne, *The Secret* (New York: Atria Books, 2006), pp. 3-4.

2. Byrne, *The Secret*, p. ix.

3. Byrne later identifies the book as *The Science of Getting Rich*, written in 1910 by Wallace Wattles.

4. "Discovering the Secret," transcript from *The Oprah Winfrey Show*, February 8, 2007, http://www.oprah.com/spiritself/slide/20070208/ss_20070208_284_101.jhtml.

5. "Making *The Secret*: A Brief History," Official Press Kit, p. 6, http://www.thesecret.tv/ts_presskit.pdf.

6. "'The Secret' to Success," Frank Mastropolo, ABC News, November 26, 2006, http://abcnews.go.com/Health/story?id=2681640&page=1.

7. Byrne, *The Secret*, p. 9.

8. *The Secret*, p. 68. Byrne states that this "Creative Process used in The Secret [ask, believe, and receive], was taken from the New Testament in the Bible…" (p. 47). This is most likely a misunderstanding or misinterpretation of Jesus' instructions in Matthew 21:22: "All things you ask in prayer, believing, you will receive." When taken in context with the rest of the New Testament, it is evident that Jesus was not teaching his followers to ask the impersonal universe to grant all their wishes. Instead, his followers were to ask Jesus for their needs in prayer for the purpose of glorifying God. "Whatever you ask in my name, that will I do, so that the Father may be glorified in the Son" (John 14:13). God is not filling orders for new cars, vacations, and houses from the great catalog of the universe. The New Testament clearly warns that God makes no promises to fulfill the requests of those asking in order to satisfy earthly desires and pleasures: "You ask and do not receive, because you ask amiss, that you may spend it on your pleasures" (James 4:3 NKJV).

9. Byrne, *The Secret*, p. 11.

10. As cited in Byrne, *The Secret*, pp. 27-28.

11. Byrne, *The Secret*, pp. 125-39. Marketing *The Secret* as a cure for cancer (along with other medical claims) has attracted a significant backlash from some within the medical community and has raised some questions concerning legal liability.

CHAPTER 3—THE SECRET CYNICS

1. Edward Mills, "Why Bad Press for *The Secret* Is Good News for Us," *Evolving Times,* March 15, 2007, http://evolvingtimes.com/2007/03/why-bad-press-for-the-secret-is-good-news-for-us.htm.

2. Jerry Adler, "Decoding 'The Secret,'" *Newsweek,* March 5, 2007, http://www.msnbc.msn.com/id/17314883/site/newsweek/page/3/.

3. Carol Memmott, " 'Secret' attracts plenty of attention," *USA TODAY,* February 14, 2007, http://www.usatoday.com/life/books/news/2007-02-14-the-secret_x.htm.

4. Peter Birkenhead, "Oprah's Ugly Secret," *Salon,* March 5, 2007, http://www.salon.com/mwt/feature/2007/03/05/the_secret/index2.html.

5. Birkenhead, "Oprah's Ugly Secret."

6. Maureen Jenkins, " 'Secret' Society," *Chicago-Sun Times,* February 23, 2007, http://www.suntimes.com/entertainment/books/269444,CST-FTR-secret23.article.

7. As cited in Rhonda Byrne, *The Secret* (New York: Atria Books, 2006), p. 128.

8. "Interview Transcript with 'Secret' Contributor Bob Proctor," ABC News *Nightline,* March 23, 2007, p. 31, http://www.abcnews.go.com/images/Nightline/Microsoft%20Word%20-%20Proctor%20Transcript.pdf.

9. "Interview Transcript," ABC News *Nightline,* p. 32.

10. Richard Hooper, "The power of positive wishful thinking," Religion and Spirituality.com, March 15, 2007, http://www.religionandspirituality.com/spirit_metaphysical/view.php?StoryID=20070315-011020-1826r.

11. "About the Authors," Sanctuary Publications Web site: http://www.sanctuarypublications.com/subjects/the-authors/the-authors.htm.

12. Jerry Adler, "Decoding 'The Secret,'" *Newsweek,* March 5, 2007, http://www.msnbc.msn.com/id/17314883/site/newsweek/page/3/.

13. Ingrid Hansen Smythe, "The Secret Behind *The Secret:* What Is Attracting Millions to the *Law of Attraction?*" eSkeptic, March 7, 2007, http://www.skeptic.com/eskeptic/07-03-07.html#note12.

14. Byrne, *The Secret,* p. 4.

15. Emily Stimpson, "Best-selling New Age 'The Secret' seen as offering only false happiness," *Our Sunday Visitor,* March 15, 2007, http://www.catholic.org/national/national_story.php?id=23402.

16. Stimpson, "Best-selling New Age 'The Secret.' "

17. Donald S. Whitney, "A Review of *The Secret* by Rhonda Byrne," http://www. spiritualdisciplines.org/secret.html.

18. From a telephone interview by the authors, March 23, 2007. Imam Kahlil is the teaching imam of the Islamic Society of Arlington, Texas.

19. Bryan Lankford, *Wicca Demystified* (New York: Marlowe & Company, 2005). Excerpt provided by the author.

20. Lankford, *Wicca Demystified.*

21. Aish HaTorah is a nonprofit, apolitical network of Jewish educational centers, with 25 branches on six continents.

22. Rabbi Benjamin Blech, "*The Secret* Revealed: God as a cosmic bellhop," published by Aish HaTorah, March 4, 2007, http://www.aish.com/societyWork/ arts/-The_Secret-_Revealed.asp.

CHAPTER 4—THE SECRET SOURCE

1. "About Abraham," http://www.abraham-hicks.com/about_abraham.php.

2. Esther Hicks and Jerry Hicks, *Ask and It Is Given: Learning to Manifest Your Desires,* http://www.abraham-hicks.com/askitisgiven_chapter_16.php.

3. Excerpted from the workshop in Kansas City, Missouri, on Sunday, August 29, 1999, http://www.abraham-hicks.com/journal.php?eid=444.

4. Allen Salkin, "Shaking Riches Out of the Cosmos," *The New York Times,* February 25, 2007, http://tinyurl.com/2hb7jc.

5. See http://www.abraham-hicks.com/102.html.

6. "Esther Hicks—Star of the Hit Movie 'The Secret,' " http://www.spiritfind.net/ jump.pl?ID=4075&Cat=Products_and_Services/Books&Dir=SpiritFind.

7. Note: The parenthetical and bracketed statements are included in the original Library of Congress description.

8. "Making *The Secret*: A Brief History," Official Press Kit, p. 6, http://www. thesecret.tv/ts_presskit.pdf.

9. Salkin, "Shaking Riches."

10. Salkin, "Shaking Riches."

11. "Jerry & Esther's Statement on 'The Secret,'" http://abrahamhicks.meetup. com/70/boards/view/viewthread?thread=2283719. Note: This statement has been removed from the official Web site (www.abraham-hicks.com) but is available upon request.

12. Salkin, "Shaking Riches," http://tinyurl.com/2hb7jc.

13. "Jerry & Esther's Statement on 'The Secret.'"

14. "Jerry & Esther's Statement on 'The Secret.'"

15. "'The Secret,' Giving and Getting, Non-Grasping, Non-Hoarding," http://integrationcoach.wordpress.com/2006/08/01/the-secret-hype/.

16. "Esther Hicks Edited from 'The Secret'?" http://thesecret.powerfulintentions.com/forum/thesecret/message-view/5140329.

17. "Esther Hicks Edited from 'The Secret'?"

18. Rhonda Byrne, *The Secret* (New York: Atria Books, 2006), pp. xiii-xv.

19. "About Us," http://www.abraham-hicks.com/about_us.php.

20. Excerpted exactly as quoted from the workshop in Portland, Oregon on Saturday, July 12, 2003, http://www.abraham-hicks.com/journal.php?eid=90.

21. "A Message from Jerry & Esther: Jul/Aug/Sep 2006," http://www.abraham-hicks.com/journal.php.

22. Esther and Jerry Hicks, *Ask and It Is Given*, pp. xxi-xxii.

23. Hicks, *Ask and It Is Given*, p. xxiii.

24. Hicks, *Ask and It Is Given*, p. xxiv.

25. Hicks, *Ask and It Is Given*, p. xxiv. Note: *Clairaudience* is "a popular form of spiritualism involving the alleged ability to hear, in a manner beyond natural explanation, paranormal phenomena such as ghosts or spirit guides" (James K. Walker, *The Concise Guide to Today's Religions and Spirituality*, Eugene, OR: Harvest House Publishers, 2007).

26. Hicks, *Ask and It Is Given*, p. xxv.

27. Hicks, *Ask and It Is Given*, p. xxvi.

28. Hicks, *Ask and It Is Given*,, p. xxvii.

29. http://www.abraham-hicks.com.

30. Excerpted from the workshop in Spokane, Washington, on Saturday, June 27, 1998, http://www.abraham-hicks.com/journal.php?eid=599.

31. Excerpted from the workshop in Silver Spring, Maryland, on Saturday, October 20, 2001, http://www.abraham-hicks.com/journal.php?eid=245.

32. This phrase is borrowed from the sci-fi classic *Star Trek: the Next Generation*. A "collective" of multiple consciousnesses functioning as one entity, the Borg, taunt individuals who resist assimilation into the collective with the phrase,

"Resistance is futile."

33. Excerpted from the workshop in Portland, Oregon, on Saturday, July 12, 2003, http://www.abraham-hicks.com/journal.php?eid=100.

CHAPTER 5—THE SECRET SÉANCE

1. E-mail from John Klimo to James Walker of excerpt from the introduction of Klimo and Pam Heath, *Suicide: What Really Happens in the Afterlife: Channeled Messages from the Dead* (Berkeley, CA: North Atlantic Books, 2006).

2. Excerpted from the workshop in Kansas City, Missouri, on Sunday, August 29, 1999, http://www.abraham-hicks.com/journal.php?eid=90.

3. Human possession by spirits other than the Holy Spirit and communication with the dead (necromancy) by anyone except God are forbidden in the Bible. Warnings are also given for demonic spirits called "familiar spirits" (e.g., Leviticus 20:27; Deuteronomy 18:9-14; 1 Samuel 28; 1 Chronicles 10:13; 2 Chronicles 33:6; Acts 16:16-18). Evil spirits often masquerade as attractive, benign messengers or "angels of light" (2 Corinthians 11:14).

4. One of the most important organizations of professional skeptics is Committee for the Scientific Investigation of Claims of the Paranormal (CSICOP). Founded in 1976 to investigate paranormal and fringe science claims from a scientific point of view, they publish *Skeptical Inquirer* magazine (see http://www.csicop. org).

5. In the interview with James Walker (April 5, 2007), Klimo described his own experiences in channeling as involving an altered state of consciousness or "self-transcendent state," in which no separate personality is manifest but there is an unmistakable awareness that something or someone else is in control of his speech. Contacting the "mind at large" in a form of "clairparlance," his speech reportedly becomes noticeably more rapid, articulate, and precise.

6. Jon Klimo, *Channeling: Investigations on Receiving Information from Paranormal Sources* (Los Angeles: Jeremy P. Tarcher, Inc. and St. Martin's Press, 1988), p. 2.

7. Klimo, *Channeling*, pp. 205-53.

8. Klimo, *Channeling*, p. 11.

9. Klimo, *Channeling*, p. 183.

CHAPTER 6—THE SECRET "BLEEP"

1. As cited in Rhonda Byrne, *The Secret* (New York: Atria Books, 2006), pp. 20-21.

2. Sometimes spelled *What the #$*! Do We Know!?* In 2006, a longer director's

cut titled *What the Bleep!?: Down the Rabbit Hole* was released. The extended edition, usually abbreviated *What the Bleep!?* contains additional commentary, animation, and several extra hours of interview footage that did not appear in the original theatrical edition.

3. Lemuria is a fictional country popularized by the discredited psychic and medium Madame Helena Petrovna Blavatsky (1831–1891), who cofounded the Theosophical Society http://www.watchman.org/profile/psychicspro.htm.

4. Otto Friedrich, "New Age Harmonies," *Time,* December 7, 1987, http://www.time.com/time/magazine/article/0,9171,966129-7,00.html.

5. "JZ Knight," Wikipedia, http://en.wikipedia.org/wiki/JZ_Knight#_note-0.

6. JZ Knight, *Ramtha, Voyage to the New World* (New York: Ballantine, 1985), p. 22. Streaming video of JZ Knight channeling Ramtha is available on Knight's Web site at http://ramtha.com/images/products/video/v1.40.ram.

7. *What the Bleep Do We Know!?* film.

8. A major focus of the meeting was brainstorming ways to put pressure on China to allow for a free and independent Tibet. "Synopsis," Dalai Lama Renaissance Web site, http://www.dalailamafilm.com/synopsis.html.

9. "Interesting Facts," Dalai Lama Renaissance Web site, http://www.dalailamafilm.com/facts.html.

10. *What the Bleep!?* film.

CHAPTER 7—THE SECRET SCIENCE

1. Rhonda Byrne, *The Secret* (New York: Atria Books, 2006), p. 15.

2. Byrne, *The Secret,* p. 156.

3. See http://www.monicalevin.com/famous-people/michael-beckwith.htm.

4. Feng shui is the ancient Chinese practice of directing spiritual energy, called *chi,* by placing and arranging objects in space according with certain religious beliefs including astrology, and yin and yang.

5. Byrne, *The Secret,* p. 197.

6. Walsch describes the process in this way: "It's not channeling or automatic writing, but more like taking dictation. What it feels like is someone whispering into my right ear. There is a voice inside my head, a voiceless voice saying things to me, and I write down what's being said, literally one sentence at a time." Sirona Knight and Michael Starwyn, "An Interview with author Neale Donald Walsch," http://www.dcsi.net/~bluesky/nwalsch1.htm.

7. Natural Law Party official Web site: http://www.natural-law.org/introduction/index.html.

8. U.S. District court, District of New Jersey (Malnak v. Yogi, D.C. Civil Action No. 76-0341), later upheld by the U.S. Court of Appeals, 3rd Circuit (Nos. 78-1568, 78-1882, 592 F. 2d 195).

9. Jeff Bloch, "We got mantras right here in River City," *Forbes*, March 24, 1986, p. 78.

10. Steve Twomey, "It's only a Short Hop to Nirvana," *Washington Post*, August 18, 1989, p. 2.

11. Catholic Msgr. Michael Ledwith served as president of St Patrick's College at Maynooth until he resigned in 1994, "amid allegations that he had been engaged in sexual harassment of students." In 2005, Irish Catholic bishops issued a report admitting that the leadership ignored complaints about Ledwith's "theological novelties" and sexual harassment at the national seminary at Maynooth in Ireland. "Irish Bishops apologize to Seminary Whistle-Blower," http://www.freerepublic.com/focus/f-religion/1427033/posts.

12. Gregory Mone, "Cult Science: Dressing up mysticism as quantum physics," *Popular Science*, October 2004, http://www.popsci.com/popsci/science/463c0b4511b84010vgnvcm1000004eecbccdrcrd.html.

13. John Gorenfeld, "The Bleep of Faith," *Salon*, September 16, 2004, http://dir.salon.com/story/ent/feature/2004/09/16/bleep/index.html?pn=1.

14. "Dr. Quantum," an animated character in the documentary *What the Bleep!?*

15. As cited in Byrne, *The Secret,* p. 160.

Chapter 8—Subatomic Thinking

1. Rhonda Byrne, *The Secret,* (New York: Atria Books, 2006), p. 156.

2. Interview with James K. Walker, April 3, 2007.

3. Byrne, *The Secret,* pp. 156-57.

4. Werner Heisenberg (1901–1976) published his theory of quantum mechanics in 1925 and was awarded the Nobel Peace Prize for physics in 1932.

5. Byrne, *The Secret,* p. 15.

6. Byrne, *The Secret,* p. 62.

7. *The Oprah Winfrey Show,* February 8, 2007.

8. As cited in Byrne, *The Secret,* pp. 20-21.

CHAPTER 9—SECRET MEDICINE

1. As cited in Rhonda Byrne, *The Secret* (New York: Atria Books, 2006), p. 128.

2. Byrne, *The Secret*, p. 14. It is never made clear why this benevolent, all-powerful, and all-knowing Universe finds it impossible to understand simple words. Apparently the Universe can comprehend the more complex ideas such as BMWs, new vacation homes, and world peace, but it struggles with the simple vocabulary of toddlers—*no, not*, and *don't*.

3. Byrne, *The Secret*, p. 59.

4. Byrne, *The Secret*, p. 60.

5. Byrne, *The Secret*, p. 61.

6. Jerry Adler, "Decoding 'The Secret,'" *Newsweek*, March 5, 2007, http://www.msnbc.msn.com/id/17314883/site/newsweek/.

7. Byrne, *The Secret*, p. 130.

8. Byrne, *The Secret*, p. 129.

9. As cited in Byrne, *The Secret*, pp. 128-29.

10. As cited in Byrne, *The Secret*, p. 134.

11. Byrne, *The Secret*, p. 135.

12. Byrne, *The Secret*, p. 131.

13. This telephone interview was conducted March 28, 2007 by Phillip Arnn, senior researcher at Watchman Fellowship, Inc.

14. Robert M. Bowman, *The Word-Faith Controversy: Understanding the Health and Wealth Gospel* (Grand Rapids: Baker Books, 2001), p. 220.

15. As cited in Byrne, *The Secret*, pp. 27-28.

16. "Double Bind: A mental or psychological dilemma caused when a person receives conflicting messages or 'truths' from a single source, leaving them unsure of the appropriate response to an issue." James K. Walker, *The Concise Guide to Today's Religions and Spirituality* (Eugene, OR: Harvest House Publishers, 2007), p. 130.

17. This is one of many aspects of *The Secret* that is paralleled in the teachings of some of the more controversial television evangelists. Media ministers such as Kenneth Copeland, Benny Hinn, and the late Kenneth Hagin teach a prosperity health-and-wealth gospel that finds much in common with Byrne's message. Viewed with skepticism by most traditional Christians, these Word-Faith teachers preach that the faithful can speak prosperity into existence out of

nothing through "positive confession." "Negative confession" generates poverty and sickness by the creative power of the human tongue. For further study, see Robert M. Bowman, *The Word-Faith Controversy: Understanding the Health and Wealth Gospel* (Grand Rapids, MI: Baker Books, 2001).

Chapter 10—Secret Consequences

1. As cited in Rhonda Byrne, *The Secret* (New York: Atria Books, 2006), p. 128. Despite the book's testimonials and repeated statements that right thinking can cure disease, *The Secret* contains an explicit disclaimer on the copyright page. It states, in part, "The information contained in this book is intended to be educational and not for diagnosis, prescription, or treatment of any health disorder whatsoever.... The author and publisher are in no way liable for any misuse of the material."

2. Byrne, *The Secret,* p. 134.

3. Byrne, *The Secret,* p. 131.

4. Byrne, *The Secret,* p. 139.

5. Byrne, *The Secret,* p. 126.

6. "Interview Transcript with 'Secret' Contributor Bob Proctor," ABC News *Nightline,* March 23, 2007, p. 31.

7. John Gorenfeld, "The Bleep of Faith," *Salon,* September 16, 2004, http://dir.salon.com/story/ent/feature/2004/09/16/bleep/index.html?pn=1. The deprogrammer testifying was Joe Szimhart, not Tom.

8. Byrne, *The Secret,* pp. xiii-xv.

9. For an overview on Christian Science, see Watchman Fellowship's profile on Christian Science at http://www.watchman.org/profile/ChrSciProfile.htm.

10. Jeffrey Ressner, "*The Secret* of Success," *Time,* December 28, 2006, http://www.time.com/time/arts/article/0,8599,1573136,00.html.

11. "The Birth of Unity," Unity of Kent, http://www.unityofkent.org/birthofunity.html.

12. *Insight,* June 20, 1988, p. 57. All four of these examples are cited in Rick Branch, "Christian Science: Healing unto Death," *The Watchman Expositor,* vol. 6, no. 8, 1989.

13. *El Paso Times,* December 6, 1988, p. 6-A.

14. The *Press Democrat,* Santa Rosa, California, April 12, 1989, p. B-3.

15. The *Press Democrat,* p. B-3.

16. "Faith Healing Harms Children," EP News, http://www.watchman.org/expo/15_2news.htm. The official Web site for CHILD, Inc. is http://www.childrenshealthcare.org.

CHAPTER 11—THE SECRET STARTER

1. Rhonda Byrne, *The Secret* (New York: Atria Books, 2006), p. ix.

2. Byrne, *The Secret,* p. 76.

3. Wallace Wattles, *The Science of Getting Rich,* http://wallacewattles.wwwhubs.com/rich.htm, Preface.

4. "Discovering The Secret," transcript from *The Oprah Winfrey Show,* February 8, 2007.

5. Jerry Adler, "Decoding the Secret," *Newsweek,* March 5, 2007. (www.msnbc.msn.com/id/17314883/site/newsweek/).

6. "Wallace Wattles: Pioneer Success Writer," http://wallacewattles.wwwhubs.com.

7. Wattles, *The Science of Getting Rich,* Chapter 5.

8. "Wallace Wattles: Pioneer Success Writer."

9. "Wallace Wattles: Pioneer Success Writer."

10. Wattles, *The Science of Getting Rich,* Chapter 6.

11. Byrne, *The Secret,* p. 9.

12. Wattles, *The Science of Getting Rich,* Chapter 5.

13. Wattles, *The Science of Getting Rich,* Chapter 5.

14. Byrne, *The Secret,* pp. 103-04.

15. Much, though not all, of the distinctive theology of the Word-Faith movement is derived from the writings of E.W. Kenyon (1867–1948)…[who was]…exposed to New Thought and Christian Science in Boston, the extent of the influence of these mind sciences (which are clearly heretical) is disputed even among Kenyon's critics. Kenyon's lasting legacy has been felt largely through his influence on popular teachers of the "Latter-Rain" movement, a "healing" revival of the late 1940s and 1950s spearheaded by the heretical and highly controversial William Branham. One of the evangelists on the fringe of that movement was Kenneth E. Hagin (1917–2003). By 1950 Hagin had started reading Kenyon's books and adopting some of Kenyon's teachings as his own. The Word-Faith movement quickly grew in size and visibility, especially through the exposure provided by the Trinity Broadcasting Network, a TV network started by Paul Crouch in 1973. That same year Kenneth Copeland Ministries was founded;

Copeland is widely regarded as the second most important teacher in the movement after Hagin. The movement's most visible and influential teachers today emphasize prosperity and general well-being and deemphasize, though not deny, the movement's controversial theology. The new generation of Word-Faith teachers includes Joyce Meyer and Joel Osteen, both of whom (unlike Hagin or Copeland) are authors of best-selling books aggressively marketed to the general public. Adapted from "Word-Faith Movement Profile" by Robert M. Bowman Jr., *Watchman Fellowship's Profile Notebook.*

16. Charles Capps, *The Tongue a Creative Force* (Tulsa, OK: Harrison House, 1976), p. 160.

17. Peter Birkenhead, "Oprah's Ugly Secret," *Salon,* March 5, 2007, www.salon.com/mwt/feature/2007/03/05/the_secret/index2.html.

18. "One Week Later: The Huge Reaction to The Secret," transcript from *The Oprah Winfrey Show,* February 16, 2007.

19. Byrne, *The Secret,* p. 17.

20. Capps, *The Tongue a Creative Force,* pp. 141-42.

21. Byrne, *The Secret,* pp. x-xi.

22. Wattles, *The Science of Getting Rich,* Chapter 10.

23. Wattles, *The Science of Getting Rich,* Chapter 10.

24. Wattles, *The Science of Getting Rich,* Chapter 10.

25. "Discovering The Secret," transcript from *The Oprah Winfrey Show,* February 8, 2007.

CHAPTER 12—THE SECRET ARCHITECTS

1. Rhonda Byrne, *The Secret* (New York: Atria Books, 2006), p. 81.

2. Charles Haanel, *The Master Key System,* http://www.consciouslivingfoundation.org/ebooks/new7/CLF-MasterKeySystem-CharlesHaanel.pdf, p. 89.

3. Byrne, *The Secret,* pp. xiii-xv.

4. Byrne, *The Secret,* p. xiv.

5. New Thought is a religious movement that developed in the nineteenth century with Phineas Parkhurst Quimby (see chapter 10), who is generally recognized as one of its originators, if not the founder. However, without question, the men and women who were central to the foundations of this movement were also influenced by Transcendentalism, promoted by popular authors of the day such as Ralph Waldo Emerson and Charles Thoreau. New Thought would spawn

many organized religions, some of which are still in existence today. These include the better known Christian Science, Unity School of Christianity, and Religious Science. The prevailing view of New Thought is monism—all is one (see chapter 16), which is common to the repeatedly expressed view of *Secret* teachers that there is a universal energy.

6. Byrne, *The Secret,* p. 152.

7. Prentice Mulford: New Thought Pioneer, http://prenticemulford.wwwhubs.com/index.html.

8. *The God in You* can be read online at http://prenticemulford.wwwhubs.com/tgiy.htm.

9. As cited in Byrne, *The Secret,* p. 66.

10. Byrne, *The Secret,* p. 66.

11. *Biography of Robert Collier,* Robert Collier Publications, http://www.robertcollier publications.com/bio.cgh.

12. Byrne, *The Secret,* p. 188.

13. Byrne, *The Secret,* p. 150.

14. Byrne, *The Secret,* p. 157.

15. As cited in Byrne, *The Secret,* pp. 157-58.

16. Haanel, *The Master Key System,* p. 38.

17. Haanel, *The Master Key System,* p. 65.

18. Haanel, *The Master Key System,* p. 88.

19. Haanel, *The Master Key System,* p. 115.

20. Byrne, *The Secret,* pp. 156-57.

21. William W. Atkinson, *Thought Vibration,* Chapter 1, http://website.lineone.net/~cornerstone2/tvib.htm#1 (emphasis in original).

22. Atkinson, *Thought Vibration,* Chapter 1.

23. Atkinson, *Thought Vibration,* Chapter 2.

24. William W. Atkinson, *Practical Mental Influence,* http://www.wisdomstore.us/downloads/Practical_Mental_Influence.pdf.

25. Atkinson, *Practical Mental Influence.*

26. Atkinson, *Practical Mental Influence.*

27. Atkinson, *Practical Mental Influence.*

28. Atkinson, *Practical Mental Influence.*

29. The numerous Internet biographies of Atkinson's life reveal he was a lawyer by profession. He became a prolific writer and activist after being introduced to New Thought through an association with Christian Science. He was the editor of *New Thought* magazine from 1901–1905 and also founded his own psychic club and the Atkinson School of Mental Science. While the editor of *New Thought,* he became interested in Hinduism and subsequently wrote a number of books devoted to Hinduism using the pseudonym Yogi Ramacharaka.

30. Wattles, *The Science of Getting Rich,* Chapter 10.

31. Wattles, *The Science of Getting Rich,* Preface.

32. Wattles, *The Science of Getting Rich,* Chapter 4.

33. Wattles, *The Science of Getting Rich,* Chapter 4.

Chapter 13—The Secret Link

1. Rhonda Byrne, *The Secret* (New York: Atria Books, 2006), p.152.

2. As cited in Byrne *The Secret,* p. 19.

3. "Discovering The Secret," transcript from *The Oprah Winfrey Show,* February 8, 2007.

4. "Discovering The Secret."

5. Byrne, *The Secret,* p. x.

6. "Discovering The Secret."

7. Agape Live, "About Dr. Michael Bernard Beckwith," http://www.agapelive.com/index.php?page=3.

8. "About the Author: Michael Beckwith," http://www.amazon.com/Change-Your-Life-Ernest-Holmes/dp/1558746862/ref=sr_1_2/002-0966843-0987201?ie=UTF8&s=books&qid=1176753057&sr=1-2.

9. Agape Live, "About Agape International Spiritual Center," http://www.agapelive.com/index.php?anchor=about.

10. "Discovering The Secret."

11. Agape Live, http://www.agapelive.com/index.php?page=3.

12. Agape Live, FAQ, http://www.agapelive.com/index.php?page=7.

13. "Ernest Holmes, Founder of the Religious Science Movement," http://ernestholmes.wwwhubs.com/.

14. "Dr. Ernest Holmes: The First Religious Scientist," by James Reid, http://www.religiousscience.org/ucrs_site/our_founder/first_religious.html.

15. The magazine was originally titled *Religious Science* but was changed in 1929 to its present title.

16. "Dr. Ernest Holmes: The First Religious Scientist."

17. "An Interview with Rev. Dr. Michael Bernard Beckwith," by Kathy Juline, http://www.newthoughtcrs.org/visioning10.htm.

18. As cited in Byrne, *The Secret,* pp. 52-53.

19. As cited in Byrne, *The Secret,* p. 164.

20. As cited in Byrne, *The Secret,* p. 170.

21. "One Week Later: The Huge Reaction to The Secret," transcript from *The Oprah Winfrey Show,* February 16, 2007.

22. "Discovering The Secret."

CHAPTER 14—SIX DEGREES OF HAANEL

1. Rhonda Byrne, *The Secret* (New York: Atria Books, 2006), p. 157.

2. Charles Haanel, *The Master Key system,* p. 14, http://www.consciouslivingfoundation.org/ebooks/new7/CLF-MasterKeySystem-CharlesHaanel.pdf.

3. "Six Degrees of Kevin Bacon," http://en.wikipedia.org/wiki/Six_Degrees_of_Kevin_Bacon.

4. Byrne, *The Secret,* p. 194.

5. Napoleon Hill claimed to have received the "Supreme Secret" directly from the voice of a disembodied spirit he called "the Master," who represented the "Venerable Brotherhood of Ancient Egypt" and claimed he was one of many "strange beings" or "unseen friends [that] hover around me, unknowable to ordinary senses." The voice of this invisible spirit being came to Hill to dictate the last chapter of his 1967 book *Grow Rich! with Peace of Mind* (New York: Ballantine Books, 1996) pp. 169-71. Hill also claimed to have communications with "the unseen Guides," who required both "gratitude for their services" and strict obedience or else disaster would follow (Napoleon Hill, *You Can Work Your Own Miracles* [Greenwich, CT: Fawcett Publications, 1971] pp. 54-55). Hill also reported imaginary nightly meetings with famous dead men whom he called his "Invisible Counselors," including "Emerson, Paine, Edison, Darwin, Lincoln, Burbank, Napoleon, Ford, and Carnegie." These meetings seemed so real he became "fearful of their consequences, and discontinued them for several months" (Napoleon Hill, *Think and Grow Rich* [New York: Fawcett Crest, 1960],

pp. 314-15, 320).

6. "Did Haanel Influence Think and Grow Rich?" http://www.haanel.com/.

7. As cited in Byrne, *The Secret*, p. 56.

8. As cited in Byrne, *The Secret*, p. 6.

9. http://www.canfieldtrainings.com/.

10. Napoleon Hill, http://en.wikipedia.org/wiki/Napoleon_Hill.

11. As cited in Byrne, *The Secret*, p. 40.

12. Byrne, *The Secret*, p. 197.

13. "Communicating with God," an interview with Neale Donald Walsch by Ravi Dykema, http://www.nexuspub.com/articles/2000/mar2000/walsch.htm.

14. "est and Werner Erhard," http://skepdic.com/est.html.

15. As cited in Byrne, *The Secret*, p. 177.

16. Byrne, *The Secret*, p. 195.

17. James Ray, *The Science of Success* (Carlsbad, CA: Sun Ark Press, 1999), p. 102.

18. Ray, *Science of Success*, p. 102.

19. Ray, *Science of Success*, p. 133.

20. As cited in Byrne, *The Secret*, pp. 45-46.

21. Jerry Adler, "Does this Self-Help Book Really Help?" *Newsweek*, March 5, 2007, http://www.msnbc.msn.com/id/17314883/site/newsweek/.

22. Wallace Wattles, *The Science of Getting Rich*, http://wallacewattles.wwwhubs.com/rich.htm, Preface.

23. Wattles, *The Science of Getting Rich*, chapter 4.

24. Adler, "Does this Self Help Book Really Help?" http://www.msnbc.msn.com/id/17314883/site/newsweek/.

25. Peter Birkenhead, "Oprah's Ugly Secret," *Salon*, March 5, 2007, www.salon.com/mwt/feature/2007/03/05/the_secret/index2.html.

CHAPTER 15—OPRAH'S SECRET ADVENTURE

1. "One Week Later: The Huge Reaction to The Secret," transcript from *The Oprah Winfrey Show*, February 16, 2007.

2. Peter Birkenhead, "Oprah's Ugly Secret," *Salon*, March 5, 2007, http://www.salon.com/mwt/feature/2007/03/05/the_secret/index2.html.

3. "Discovering The Secret," transcript from *The Oprah Winfrey Show*, February 8, 2007.

4. "One Week Later: The Huge Reaction to The Secret."

5. Birkenhead, "Oprah's Ugly Secret."

6. "Discovering The Secret."

7. As cited in Rhonda Byrne, *The Secret* (New York: Atria Books, 2006), pp. 13-14.

8. As cited in Byrne, *The Secret*, p. 20.

9. "Discovering The Secret."

10. "Discovering The Secret."

11. "Discovering The Secret."

12. "Lady with a Calling," *Time*, August 8, 1988, http://www.time.com/time/magazine/article/0,9171,968069,00.html.

13. "Oprah's Favorite Books," http://www2.oprah.com/books/favorite/books_favorite_main.jhtml.

14. "Oprah's Favorite Books."

15. "Oprah's Favorite Books."

16. Oprah Winfrey, *The Uncommon Wisdom of Oprah*, ed. Bill Adler (New York: Carol Publishing Group, 1997), p. 234.

17. "One Week Later: The Huge Reaction to The Secret."

18. "This Month's Mission," *O, The Oprah Magazine*, May 2004, http://www.oprah.com/omagazine/200405/omag_200405_mission.jhtml.

19. "This Month's Mission," *O, The Oprah Magazine*, January 2004, http://www.oprah.com/omagazine/200401/omag_200401_mission.jhtml.

20. "Meditation with Oprah," http://www.oprah.com/spiritself/insp/med/ss_insp_med_lybloprah.jhtml.

21. "One Week Later: The Huge Reaction to The Secret."

22. "One Week Later."

23. Oprah, *The Uncommon Wisdom of Oprah*, p. 233.

24. Oprah, *The Uncommon Wisdom of Oprah*, p. 239.

25. "What Do You Believe?" *The Oprah Winfrey Show*, January 30, 1996.

26. LaTonya Taylor, "The Church of O," *Christianity Today*, April 2, 2002, p. 38.

CHAPTER 16—THE SACRED SECRET

1. Rhonda Byrne, *The Secret* (New York: Atria Books, 2006), p. 182.

2. Byrne, *The Secret,* p. 175.

3. As cited in Byrne, *The Secret,* p. 164.

4. Paraphrase of the serpent's promises to Eve in the Garden of Eden—see Genesis 3:1-5 in the Bible.

5. As cited in Byrne, *The Secret,* p. 160.

6. Byrne, *The Secret,* p. 164.

7. Rabbi Benjamin Blech, "The Secret Revealed: God as a cosmic bellhop," published by Aish HaTorah, March 4, 2007, http://www.aish.com/societyWork/arts/-The_Secret-_Revealed.asp.

8. Jack Mason, the owner of two general-market bookstores, Books for Less, north of Atlanta, Georgia, has refused to carry *The Secret* because of its anti-Christian message. (CBA/Aspiring Retail e-newsletter April 10, 2007, originally reported in the *Gwinnett Daily Post* (of Gwinnett County, Georgia).

9. Byrne, *The Secret,* p. 183.

10. Donald S. Whitney, "A Review of *The Secret* by Rhonda Byrne," http://www.spiritualdisciplines.org/secret.html.

11. Byrne, *The Secret,* p. 177.

12. As cited in Byrne, *The Secret,* p. 183.

13. Genesis 3:1-5 in the Bible.

ABOUT WATCHMAN FELLOWSHIP

Watchman Fellowship, founded in 1979, is one of America's largest Christian discernment ministries and provides research, education, and outreach for individuals involved with new religious movements, cults, and the occult. With offices in seven states and missionaries in Eastern Europe, we maintain a research library of over 50,000 cataloged resources (including files, books, periodicals, and media) and an award-winning Web site, www.watchman.org. Teaching in hundreds of churches, colleges, and universities annually, we help tens of thousands to understand biblical Christianity as contrasted to new religious movements, cults, the occult, and New Age spirituality. We are recognized by the media as trusted experts and have been interviewed on *Nightline, World News Tonight, The NewsHour with Jim Lehrer,* and *USA Today.* For contact information, visit www.watchman.org.